Called to Witness and Service

GS 1329

Conversations between
The British and Irish Anglican Churches
and
The French Lutheran and Reformed Churches

CALLED TO WITNESS AND SERVICE

The Reuilly Common Statement
with
Essays on Church, Eucharist and Ministry

CHURCH HOUSE PUBLISHING

Church House Publishing
Church House
Great Smith Street
London
SW1P 3NZ

ISBN 07151 5757 4

Published 1999 for the Church of England's Council for Christian Unity
by Church House Publishing

Printed in England by Halstan & Co Ltd.

Contents

Contents

Conversations between
The British and Irish Anglican Churches
and
The French Lutheran and Reformed Churches

THE REUILLY COMMON STATEMENT

Contents

Notes

Biblical quotations are from the *New Revised Standard Version*.

The English and French texts are equally definitive.

Foreword

by the Co-Chairmen

A Fruit of the Ecumenical Movement

1.   Our time is full of openings and promise for our churches. The World Council of Churches, which celebrates its fiftieth anniversary this year, is part of the Ecumenical Movement working for reconciliation, understanding and new confidence between many churches throughout the world. The Ecumenical Movement has spurred the conviction in the churches that they can and must make progress towards unity. This conviction has led to significant inter-church dialogues which have brought new openings in the search for visible unity.

2.   Anglicans have been engaged in a number of theological conversations with the churches of the Lutheran World Federation and the World Alliance of Reformed Churches both at global and regional levels. These dialogues and relationships, as well as the wider ecumenical convergence with other ecumenical partners and multilaterally in the work of the Faith and Order Commission of the World Council of Churches, have encouraged the British and Irish Anglican churches and the French Lutheran and Reformed churches to seek a closer relationship.

Sociological and Historical Motivations

3.   Furthermore, the great upheavals in which Europe has been living since 1989 (the end of the division of Europe into East and West and the speeding-up of the building of Europe) have resulted in a desire for openness, for relations and for exchange between peoples. Finally, the opening of the Channel Tunnel, a highly symbolic technological achievement, has led to an unprecedented rapprochement between the British Isles and the Continent. For these reasons, the Anglican presence in France and the Lutheran and Reformed presence in Great Britain and Ireland are bound to develop. The churches cannot ignore these factors, and could not but respond to them by new openings on this level between our respective countries.

The Initial Impulse – the Spirit of Dialogue

4.   Moreover the German Protestant churches and the Church of England began a dialogue which led to the Meissen Agreement; this produced lively interest among French Lutheran and Reformed churches, and a desire to take steps towards closer fellowship with their Anglican partner-churches from across the Channel. This would give concrete closer expression for our churches of the rapprochement achieved through international dialogues. When the then Archbishop of Canterbury, Dr Robert Runcie, visited Strasbourg in November 1989, this issue was put to the Archbishop by the President of the Standing Council of the Lutheran and Reformed Churches (CPLR), at the request of his Council.

5.   The Church of England did not think that it was appropriate simply to encourage the French Lutheran and Reformed churches to sign the Meissen Agreement. While the Church of England is the established church, in France, the Protestant churches (except in Alsace) have been described as being in 'diaspora'; overall, French Protestants form a small minority. Nor are there the number of local twinnings which characterized the background to the Meissen Agreement. This called for a particular dialogue. With the agreement of the other British and Irish Anglican churches to take part, this particularity intensified because Scottish and Irish Anglicans can also be said to be minority churches in a diaspora situation, while Welsh Anglicans bring another experience of former state establishment. On the other hand, it was felt important to work in continuity with the Meissen Agreement and the Porvoo Agreement (between the British and Irish Anglican churches and the Nordic and Baltic Lutheran churches), in order to maintain a consistency with what has been agreed between Anglicans and Lutherans and Reformed in Europe.

6.   After initial contacts, a preliminary session in September 1992, at the house of the deaconess community in Versailles, outlined the issues which this dialogue would have to consider. The conversations were most promising, albeit not without difficulties.

7.   The promise lay in the mutual discovery that two traditions, Anglican and Lutheran/Reformed, belong to the same European Christian community, as well as in the interest shown in forming closer relations on both sides of the Channel. On the occasion of his visit to Strasbourg (November 1989) Dr Runcie drew attention to the important past links

between our Churches.[1] It would not have seemed strange in any way to Anglicans and French-speaking Lutherans and Reformed in the sixteenth, seventeenth or even eighteenth centuries to wish to establish a closer fellowship together, even though there were acknowledged differences of church order, particularly regarding the episcopate, with varying evaluations of the desirability or necessity of episcopacy among theologians in Britain and Ireland and in France. There was a certain ecclesial recognition in spite of acknowledged problems about the interchangeability of ministers between episcopal and non-episcopal churches. The Continental Protestant churches were generally regarded in a different light from churches in England which did not have bishops.

8.   The differences experienced were due to two main factors:

•   A theological or ecclesiological disparity between the Anglican and the French Protestant churches. Anglicans have a strong, firmly structured ecclesiology in which questions of the ministry and of episcopal succession are of great importance, all the more so since they are under discussion within the church itself. The French Protestant churches, often for reasons of their long history with a dominant Roman Catholic Church, are reticent to emphasize these very questions in any way, and often approach them in very different ways.

•   The numerical, sociological and juridical disparity between the churches concerned (cf. Common Statement, para. 4). This disparity will, in any case, require a specific and realistic re-appraisal of our concrete relations (cf. para. 15 below).

9.   The dialogue was undertaken seriously. It has led to the present results because the promises seemed to be more important than the difficulties. The unity which we have received in our common faithfulness to Christ and in our common engagement in mission has allowed us to see even these difficulties as promising challenges rather than as barriers which will keep us separated for ever. It was with this conviction that we started our dialogue.

---

[1]   Cf. C. Hill and J.-P. Monsarrat, 'An Outline of our Relationships', appended to the Common Statement.

The Course of our Work

10.   The participating churches (the French Lutheran and Reformed churches united in the CPLR and the Anglican churches of Great Britain and Ireland) nominated their official delegates and agreed observers who were to be associated with the work.[2] A debt of gratitude must be expressed to our observers: from the Leuenberg Church Fellowship, Dr Wilhelm Hüffmeier; from the United Reformed Church in the United Kingdom, the Revd Fleur Houston; and from the Roman Catholic Church in France, Père Christian Forster and his predecessor Père Guy Lourmande. Pasteur Jean-Pierre Monsarrat also gave both invaluable service as a Consultant and also with Fleur Houston supplied interpretation and translation services for the dialogue. The contribution of these observers and Pasteur Monsarrat cannot be overestimated and we express to them our sincere thanks.

11.   The four plenary sessions of the Commission, and an equal number of meetings of the drafting committee, produced a draft text and a number of supporting essays. On two separate occasions, committees of the participating churches were specially consulted before the final text was agreed. This was to prevent any possible major difficulty which might have arisen at a later point in the course of referring the agreement to the respective synodical processes.

12.   The result of all this work is here presented to the partner churches in this dialogue, for submission to the synodical processes.

Discoveries Made on the Way: Objectives Attained and Theological Characteristics

13.   We believe there are some distinctive theological characteristics to this dialogue. These theological characteristics give this dialogue a theological significance beyond the question of the size or context of the immediate dialogue partners. Our proposed agreement needs to be seen alongside the Meissen and Porvoo agreements as a possible basis for dialogue between Anglicans, Lutherans and Reformed in the future. It has thus a potentially wider significance than the British and Irish Anglican and the French Lutheran and Reformed churches.

---

[2]   See the list of participants on pp.41f.

14. We believe our work had achieved a significant clarification in the use of terms which are often misunderstood and used differently. This is particularly true of the different ways in which Anglicans on the one hand and Lutherans and Reformed on the other use the term 'recognition'. For Lutherans and Reformed the mutual recognition of the Church of Jesus Christ in each other, which goes together with the recognition of an authentic ministry of word and sacraments, entails reconciliation and the fullest degree of Church unity. Nevertheless, Lutheran and Reformed have come to agree that this must be implemented step by step. Anglicans speak in terms of recognition or acknowledgement of the Church of Christ in another tradition, including acknowledgement of an authentic ministry of word and sacrament, but go on to speak of a further stage of the reconciliation or uniting of ministries, a common ministry in the historic episcopal succession (cf. Common Statement, paras 26–9). Our dialogue has helped us to see how we use the same term recognition in different ways. This has enabled us to reach agreement that mutual recognition or acknowledgement of each other implies a further stage of reconciliation. For Lutheran and Reformed the emphasis will be upon increasing the visibility of what is already given in Christ; for Anglicans, there will be an emphasis on the necessity of that visibility if unity is to be full. These emphases are complementary, as will be seen from our important agreement that: 'in order to be truly itself and to fulfil its mission the Church must be seen to be one' (Common Statement, para. 21).

The Necessary Consequences

15. Finally, we also became aware of the question of how closer fellowship can be established between churches in very different socio-religious contexts and with different historical and theological backgrounds. This will require particular attention and we, the co-chairmen, commit ourselves to establishing a small working party to examine practical and realistic possibilities for the implementation of the Agreement, if accepted by our churches. This will have a somewhat different character from the widespread network of local parish contacts between Church of England parishes and German Protestant parishes. At the local level multilateral twinnings will usually be more relevant when they include the United Reformed Church and English and French Roman Catholic partners.

There could also be significant scope for examining French Lutheran and Reformed collaboration with francophone Anglican provinces in Africa and elsewhere. The Irish, Scottish and Welsh Anglican partnership will add a further dimension to our relationship, healthily challenging Church of England 'establishment' assumptions!

Why 'Reuilly Agreement'?

16. Reuilly is neither a town, like Meissen or Porvoo, nor a meeting-place like Leuenberg. It is a district of Paris, where, in the nineteenth century, a deaconesses' centre came into being, similar to the many which were flourishing in Europe at that time. Its vocation was service, witness, mission and, already, unity between the different spiritual families of Protestantism. The Deaconesses of Reuilly soon became very well known and influential in France. Later, they were one of the first Protestant communities to find a new direction for their vocation, that of contemplative prayer. In order to do this, in 1970 they established a community centre in Versailles, where they developed a life of prayer and meditation with even greater ecumenical dimensions and wider influence. This is where the first two of our sessions were held. It is in the same spirit of prayer with an ecumenical outlook that the members of the Conversations today submit the fruits of their work to the discernment of the churches who commissioned it, in the hope of fruits to come.

Two Points of Clarification for the Debates in the Synodical Structures of the Churches

17. The different parts of this agreed text do not all have the same status. Chapters I to VII as well as Chapter IX describe the context in which our dialogue took place, the bases for our agreement and the way of its implementation. Only the Declaration itself in Chapter VIII (para. 46) requires formal adoption by the synodical structures and will need to be put to a vote. The Essays, concerning the identity and some essential aspects of the life of the partner churches, are added mainly for background information.

18. If, as we sincerely hope, the synodical structures of our churches adopt the Reuilly Declaration and make it their own, this would mean

that the Anglican, Lutheran and Reformed signatory churches will have taken a decisive step forward in the direction of visible unity, and will have established between them a closer sharing in word and sacrament allowing for mutual hospitality in worship and witness. Certain significant ecclesiological questions (mentioned in para. 43) do not yet allow full interchangeability of ministries between these Anglican churches on the one hand and these Lutheran and Reformed churches on the other, but this agreement is for us a strong call to continue the dialogue and to go forward on the way to full visible unity.

19. We give thanks to God for the faithful and fraternal spirit in which our conversations took place, for the confidence which has been established between us, and for the wonderful mutual opening which the Reuilly Agreement both makes possible and calls for between the participating churches. We pray to God for the building up of his one Church through the ministries of our different churches, and we pray for our common progress towards full visible unity.

WERNER JURGENSEN

Pasteur Werner Jurgensen

President of the CPLR

✠ CHRISTOPHER STAFFORD

The Rt Revd Christopher Hill

Bishop of Stafford

I Setting the Scene

A Our Common Calling

1. Our churches share the conviction that God's Spirit is urgently calling them, together with other churches, to give visibility to their communion (*koinonia*) and, by their words and actions, to proclaim together the good news to the world.

2. We give thanks for all the blessings we have received through our own traditions, for the faith, devotion and witness, often costly, of our forebears. We long to share these with one another. We also give thanks for the ecumenical progress which has opened up new understandings, brought all our churches close, and made this particular enterprise possible. We give thanks for the signs of peace and freedom in Europe. The continuing witness and experience of churches in Ireland adds a particular dimension to our work of reconciliation.

3. In our common Christian experience we are aware of the need for the recognition of our weakness, the need to repent of our faithlessness and the need to heal our distorted attitudes and broken relationships and build wider ecumenical partnerships. We need a conversion of our churches to Christ and to one another in Christ: in turning to Christ we come closer to one another.

4. Some of our churches are comparatively large, while others are small and in some cases dispersed. They have different legal relationships with the State. In a pluralist and rapidly changing Europe, which no longer finds meaning in a predominantly Christian frame of reference, all churches experience a degree of marginalization. Many people lack a clear sense of direction, are confused by competing ideals and values, and feel powerless and alienated. We are all faced by issues of justice, peace and stewardship of God's creation. These issues have to be addressed in a deeper engagement and solidarity with people of every continent.

5. It is in this context that God calls us and offers us gifts to fulfil this urgent calling. We shall respond more faithfully if we respond together. We must no longer journey alone.

B   Our Common Experience

6.   The links between Christians in France and Britain and Ireland go back centuries before the Reformation. There were, however, close relations between the reforming theologians during the middle years of the sixteenth century. Martin Bucer, a reformer from Alsace who spent three years in England, was a friend of Thomas Cranmer and influenced his liturgical reforms.

7.   At various crucial periods during the sixteenth, seventeenth and eighteenth centuries exile and refugee communities also brought Anglicans, Lutherans and Reformed into contact with one another. English and Welsh exiles were received in Strasbourg during the persecution of Mary Tudor, and during the Commonwealth period those who remained loyal to the Prayer Book, episcopacy and the Crown fled to Paris. Huguenot refugees came to London and elsewhere in Britain and Ireland throughout the sixteenth and seventeenth centuries, especially after the Revocation of the Edict of Nantes (1685), which had hitherto protected French Reformed Christians.

8.   As the eighteenth century progressed, contact between the churches decreased and earlier friendships and recognition were almost forgotten, even if the influence of British philosophers and theologians persisted, particularly in Strasbourg. In this century closer relationships were once again established, including a series of Anglo-French Theological Conferences, in large part due to the worldwide ecumenical movement, of which Anglicans, Lutherans and Reformed are part.[1]

C   Growing Communion

9.   In this century our churches have been increasingly aware of God's desire for the unity of the Church. They were among the first to engage in world mission and to commit themselves to the Faith and Order and Life and Work movements. They were among the founding members of the World Council of Churches (WCC). Within this broad ecumenical movement they sought to overcome divisive issues and to rediscover unity in faith. The aim has always been to give a greater visibility to the unity

---

[1]   For a fuller treatment of contacts in the past, see C. Hill and J.-P. Monsarrat, 'An Outline of our Relationships', appended to this Common Statement.

of the Church of Jesus Christ. The reports of the Faith and Order Commission of the WCC, *Baptism, Eucharist and Ministry, Confessing the One Faith*, and *Church and World*, illustrate significant progress at the multilateral, international level. The network of bilateral dialogues involving Anglicans, Lutherans, Methodists, Orthodox, Reformed and Roman Catholics has to be seen in this wider multilateral context. The bilateral and multilateral dialogues are complementary; they contribute to, and receive from, one another's achievements.

10.   Among the most significant results of the international bilateral dialogues in which our churches have been involved together are: the Anglican–Reformed report *God's Reign and Our Unity* (1984);[2] Anglican–Lutheran reports such as the Pullach Report (1973),[3] the Helsinki Report (1983),[4] *The Niagara Report* (1988)[5] and *The Diaconate as Ecumenical Opportunity* (1996);[6] and the Lutheran–Reformed report *Toward Church Fellowship* (1989).[7] These texts demonstrate a fundamental consensus concerning the understanding of the gospel, the confession of faith, the word and the sacraments. We share a high degree of agreement on the understanding of the Church and its ministry which we elaborate in this text.

11.   Our Christian world communions have invited our churches to embrace the results of the dialogues and to translate them, at all levels, including the regional level, into visible expressions of the communion which is already ours. In spite of some setbacks, developments in Lutheran–Reformed–Anglican relations in recent years in Europe have been encouraging and have resulted in closer relationships.

---

[2]   *God's Reign and Our Unity. The Report of the Anglican–Reformed International Commission 1981–1984* (GROU).

[3]   *Anglican–Lutheran International Conversations. The Report of the Conversation 1970–1972 authorized by the Lambeth Conference and the Lutheran World Federation* (London, 1973) (*Pullach*), paras 17–82.

[4]   *Anglican–Lutheran Dialogue. The Report of the European Commission.* Helsinki, August–September 1982 (London, 1983) (Helsinki, paras 17–51.) Parts of the Report are reprinted in the Cold Ash Report (1983).

[5]   Anglican–Lutheran International Continuation Committee, *The Niagara Report. Report of the Anglican–Lutheran Consultation on Episcope.* Niagara Falls, September 1987 (London, 1988), paras 60–80.

[6]   *The Diaconate as Ecumenical Opportunity. The Hanover Report of the Anglican–Lutheran International Commission* (London, 1996).

[7]   *Toward Church Fellowship. The Report of the Lutheran–Reformed International Commission* (Geneva, 1989).

- The French Lutheran and Reformed churches approved the Leuenberg Agreement (1973),[8] in which European churches from these two traditions 'accord each other table and pulpit fellowship' and recognize each other as authentic expressions of the one Church of Jesus Christ. This agreement has been deepened through continuing theological dialogue and has been received and officially accepted by a growing number of churches. Through a 'common declaration', the Leuenberg signatory churches and the Methodist churches in Europe entered into church fellowship in 1996.

- The Church of England and the Lutheran, Reformed and United churches in Germany have responded to the international dialogues by entering into the Meissen Agreement (1988).[9] These German churches also participate with the French Lutheran and Reformed churches in the Leuenberg Agreement.

- The Nordic and Baltic Lutheran churches together with the Anglican churches of Britain and Ireland have entered into communion on the basis of the Porvoo Agreement.[10] This new relationship goes beyond the Meissen Agreement and establishes a common ecclesial life served by a common ministry in the historic episcopal succession.

The Leuenberg, Meissen and Porvoo Agreements provide an important foundation for this present conversation.

12. At the European level there are many related partnerships. The French Lutheran and Reformed churches enjoy 'church fellowship' with those churches in Britain and Ireland which subscribe to the Leuenberg Agreement (the United Reformed Church in the United Kingdom, the Presbyterian Church of Ireland, the Church of Scotland, the United Free Church of Scotland, the Presbyterian Church of Wales, the Lutheran Church in Ireland, and the Lutheran Church in Great Britain). Through a 'Joint Declaration of Church Fellowship' the Leuenberg signatory churches and the Methodist churches of Europe entered into communion

---

[8]   *Agreement between Reformation Churches in Europe (Leuenberg Agreement)*, ed. W. Hüffmeier (Frankfurt am Main, 1993) (*Leuenberg*).

[9]   *The Meissen Agreement. Texts* (CCU Occasional Paper No. 2, 1992).

[10]   *Together in Mission and Ministry. The Porvoo Common Statement with Essays on Church and Mission in Northern Europe* (London, 1993).

in 1996. Similarly, the Anglican churches of Britain and Ireland have, through the Bonn Agreement (1931–2), a relationship of what has been called 'full intercommunion' with the Old Catholic churches.

13. The international and European movements need to be seen in relation to the developing ecumenical relations at the national and local levels. The new agreements both benefit from concrete local experience and at the same time give impetus to further local developments. All of our churches are involved in a series of bilateral and multilateral discussions and relationships at national level, for example the informal bilateral discussion between the Church of England and the United Reformed Church.

14. In each of our countries the relationship with the Roman Catholic Church is important and our churches work together through official ecumenical structures, for example national councils of churches. In France the Lutheran and Reformed churches have for 30 years had a strong theological dialogue with the Roman Catholic Church with significant results (for example, the work of the Comité Mixte on baptism, basic consensus, ethical commitments, etc., and the work of the 'Groupe des Dombes'). Mutual eucharistic hospitality has been offered to inter-church families in the Diocese of Strasbourg. Anglican churches have had many links at different levels with the Roman Catholic Church in France as well as in England. Many of these have been fostered by the national Anglican–Roman Catholic committees (ARCs). French ARC and English ARC produced jointly the report *Twinnings and Exchanges*, which led to eucharistic hospitality being offered to individual Anglicans when they are in France.[11]

15. The relationship that would be established on the basis of this Common Statement needs to be seen and enriched within the wider network of developing relationships. It has been important to have observers from the Roman Catholic Church in France and the United Reformed Church in the United Kingdom at the present conversations.

---

[11] *Twinnings and Exchanges. Guidelines proposed by the Anglican–Roman Catholic Committees of France and England* (London, 1990).

II The Church as Sign, Instrument and Foretaste of the Kingdom of God

16. God's plan as declared in the Holy Scriptures is to reconcile all things in Christ in, through and for whom they were made.[12]

17. For this purpose, God chose Israel, sent Jesus Christ and commissioned the Church. Abraham's call was for the blessing of all peoples (Genesis 12.1-3). Israel was promised that the servant of God would not only restore the scattered people of Israel; he is given 'as a light to the nations', to bring salvation to 'the end of the earth' (Isaiah 49.6). In Christ God was reconciling the whole world to himself (2 Corinthians 5.19; Colossians 1.15-20). The Letter to the Ephesians recognizes the implications of the work of Christ for the mystery, the call and the mission of the Church, when it says 'God . . . has blessed us in Christ with every spiritual blessing . . . With all wisdom and insight he has made known to us the mystery of his will, according to his good pleasure that he set forth in Christ, as a plan for the fullness of time, to gather up all things in him, things in heaven and things on earth' (Ephesians 1.3,9,10). 'But each of us was given grace according to the measure of Christ's gift . . . The gifts he gave were that some would be apostles, some prophets, some evangelists, some pastors and teachers, to equip the saints for the work of ministry, for building up the body of Christ, until all of us come to the unity of the faith and of the knowledge of the Son of God, to maturity, to the measure of the full stature of Christ' (Ephesians 4.7,11-13).

18. The Church, the body of Christ, must always be seen in this perspective as instrumental to God's ultimate purpose. The Church exists for the glory of God and to serve, in obedience to the mission of Christ, the reconciliation of humankind and of all creation. Therefore the Church is sent into the world as a sign, instrument and foretaste of a reality which

---

[12] Paras 16–23 are based on *Meissen*, paras 1–8, and para. 31 contains quotations from *Meissen*, para. 15. Paras 33–40 reflect the convergences which have taken place since Meissen. Throughout this report we have chosen to refer to the Meissen and Porvoo Common Statements for the sake of consistency and coherence of the different ecumenical dialogues. We recognize that these matters could also be formulated differently to express the same basic biblical convictions.

comes from beyond history – the kingdom, or reign of God. It is already a provisional embodiment of God's will, which is the coming of the kingdom.[13] The Church is a divine reality, holy and transcending present finite reality. At the same time, being also a human institution, it shares all the ambiguity and frailty of the human condition, and is always called to repentance, reform and renewal.[14]

---

[13] Cf. *GROU*, para. 29f.

[14] Cf. *Helsinki*, para. 47. The assertion that the Church is a divine reality always has to be qualified by the fact that it is always called to repentance, reform and renewal, and has constantly to depend on God's mercy and forgiveness (cf. *Porvoo*, para. 20).

III The Church as Communion
(*Koinonia*)

19.   Today we are rediscovering, together with other Christians, the communal character of the Church. Underlying many of the New Testament descriptions of the Church, such as 'the people of God', 'the body of Christ', 'the bride', 'the temple of the Spirit', is the reality of a *koinonia* – a communion – with God and with one another (1 John 1.3-4). According to the Scriptures, we are introduced into this community – *koinonia* – through a baptism inseparable from faith and conversion.[15] The vocation of all the baptized is to live as a corporate priesthood offering praise to God, sharing the good news and engaging in mission and service to humankind. This common life is sustained and nurtured by God's grace through word and sacraments. It is served by the ordained ministry and also held together by other bonds of communion.[16]

20.   The Church is the community (*koinonia*) of those reconciled with God and with one another. It is the community of those who, in the power of the Holy Spirit, believe in Jesus Christ and are justified through God's grace (cf. para. 31 (c) below). The Church has a mission to be the reconciling community because it has been called to bring to all humankind God's gracious offer of redemption and renewal.[17] Because the *koinonia* is also a participation in Christ crucified, it is part of the nature and mission of the Church to share in the sufferings and struggles of humankind.

---

[15]   Cf. *Leuenberg*, para. 14.

[16]   See para. 31 (h) and (e) below. Cf. *Leuenberg*, paras 2 and 13. The Leuenberg ecclesiology was deepened in the text *The Church of Jesus Christ. The Contribution of the Reformation towards Ecumenical Dialogue on Church Unity*, ed. W. Hüffmeier (Leuenberger Texte, 1, 1995).

[17]   Cf. Anglican–Roman Catholic International Commission, *The Final Report*. Windsor September 1981 (London, 1982) (ARCIC, *Final Report*), Introduction, para. 8. Cf. *Leuenberg*, paras 11 and 36.

IV Growth Towards Full Visible Unity

21. In order to be truly itself and to fulfil its mission the Church must be seen to be one. The missionary imperative entails the overcoming of the divisions which have kept our churches apart. As our churches grow in faith into the fullness of Christ, so they will grow together in unity (Ephesians 1). This unity will reflect the different gifts God has given to his Church in many nations, languages, cultures and traditions.

22. Perfect unity must await the full realization of God's kingdom, in which all will be completely obedient to God and therefore totally reconciled to one another in God. But in a fallen world we are committed to strive for the 'full visible unity' of the body of Christ on earth.[18] We are to work for the manifestation of unity at every level, a unity which is grounded in the life of the Holy Trinity and is God's purpose for the whole of creation. All our attempts to describe this vision are bound to be provisional. We are continually being led to see fresh depths and riches of that unity and to grasp new ways in which it might be manifested in word and action. Every experience of unity is a gift of God and a foretaste and sign of the kingdom.

A The Description of Full Visible Unity

23. As the churches grow together, their understanding of the characteristics of full visible unity becomes clearer. We can already claim together that full visible unity must include:

- A common proclamation and hearing of the gospel, a common confession of the apostolic faith in word and action. That one faith has to be confessed together, locally and universally, so that God's reconciling purpose is everywhere shown forth. Living this apostolic faith, the Church helps the world to attain its proper destiny.

---

[18] This emphasis on the need for full visible unity is the emerging consensus in the ecumenical movement today. It has most recently been expressed in the Papal Encyclical *Ut Unum Sint.*

- The sharing of one baptism, the celebrating of one eucharist and the service of a common ministry (including the exercise of a ministry of oversight, *episkope*).[19] This common participation in one baptism, one eucharist and one ministry unites 'all in each place' with 'all in every place' within the whole communion of saints. In every local celebration of the eucharist the Church represents and manifests the communion of the universal Church. Through the visible communion the healing and uniting power of the Triune God is made evident amidst the divisions of humankind.

- Bonds of communion which enable the Church at every level to guard and interpret the apostolic faith, to take decisions, to teach authoritatively, to share goods and to bear effective witness in the world. The bonds of communion will possess personal, collegial and communal aspects. At every level they are outward and visible signs of the communion between persons who, through faith, baptism and eucharist, are drawn into the communion of the Triune God.[20] This communion must have practical consequences, in particular a common engagement of the churches in service and mission.[21]

24. In such communion churches are bound together in confessing the one faith and engaging in worship and witness, deliberation and action, and are united with the Church through the ages, which reaches out to its fulfilment in the coming of the kingdom of God.

25. Full visible unity should not be confused with uniformity: unity in Christ does not exist in spite of and in opposition to diversity, but is given with and in diversity.[22] Both the unity and the diversity of the Church are grounded in the Triune God, who is perfect communion in diversity. Diversities which are rooted in the biblical witness, theological traditions, spiritualities, liturgies and expressions of ministry, and in various cultural,

---

[19] Cf. para. 27 below.

[20] Cf. *Meissen*, para. 8, *Porvoo*, para. 20, Roman Catholic/Lutheran Joint Commission, *Facing Unity. Models, Forms and Phases of Catholic–Lutheran Church Fellowship* (n.pl., 1985), para. 3, and *Leuenberg*, paras 33 and 35. *Leuenberg*, para. 33 underlines the mutual recognition of ordained ministry.

[21] Cf. The Canberra Statement 'The Unity of the Church as *Koinonia*: Gift and Calling', in *Signs of the Spirit*, Official Report, WCC Seventh Assembly, ed. M. Kinnamon (Geneva, 1991), pp. 172 ff. and *Leuenberg*, para. 35.

[22] Cf. *Porvoo*, para. 23; *Leuenberg*, paras 28 and 29.

ethnic or historical contexts, are integral to the nature of communion. Yet there are limits to diversity. Diversity is illegitimate when, for instance, it makes impossible the common confession of Jesus Christ as God and Saviour the same yesterday, today and forever (Hebrews 13.8). Diversity is illegitimate when it denies salvation through Christ and the final destiny of humanity as proclaimed in Holy Scripture, preached by the apostolic community and celebrated in the liturgy of the Church. In communion diversities are brought together in harmony as gifts of the Holy Spirit, contributing to the richness and fullness of the Church of God.[23]

B Mutual Recognition on the Way to Full Visible Unity

26. On the way to full visible unity, the recognition in each other's lives of the authentic preaching of the word of God and the due celebration of the sacraments of baptism and eucharist and the acknowledgement that one another's ordained ministries are given by God as instruments of grace constitute a significant step. This enables us to recognize the presence of the Church of Jesus Christ in one another and impels us to share together in the celebration of the word and the offering and receiving of eucharistic hospitality. Moreover, communion in word and sacraments entails the mutual sharing of resources, spiritual and material, within the one Body of Christ. It also entails a communion in mission and service to the world.

27. For the Lutheran and Reformed churches this mutual recognition already expresses and signifies the unity of the Church. Mutual recognition for them entails full communion, which includes full interchangeability of ministries.[24] This given reality has to be implemented step by step. Anglicans, on the other hand, make a distinction between the recognition (acknowledgement) of the Church of Christ in another tradition, including the authentic word, sacraments and ministries of the other churches, and a further stage – the formation of a reconciled, common ministry in the historic episcopal succession, together with the establishment of forms of collegial and conciliar oversight. Anglicans speak of this further stage as 'the reconciliation of churches and ministries'.

---

[23] Cf. The Canberra Statement, para. 2.2.

[24] Cf. *Leuenberg*, para. 33.

28. Lutherans, Reformed and Anglicans agree that mutual recognition (acknowledgement) of the preaching of the word, the celebration of the sacraments and ministries impels them to continue to strive for a life of communion served by a common ministry, including the ministry of pastoral oversight (*episkope*) and bonds of conciliarity.

29. We believe that our churches are called to move together by stages to the full visible unity of the Church as a movement of the conversion of our churches in the sense of a turning to Christ and a turning to one another in Christ.[25] This conversion is the work of the Holy Spirit, who opens us up to a life beyond what we can imagine or construct.

---

[25] Groupe des Dombes, cf. *For the Conversion of the Churches* (Geneva, 1993).

V Agreement in Faith

30. The recommendations which we make in Chapter VIII are grounded in the agreed statements between representatives of the churches of the Anglican Communion and the Lutheran World Federation, and of the churches of the Anglican Communion and the World Alliance of Reformed Churches. Alongside these agreed statements must also be set the report of the Faith and Order Commission of the World Council of Churches *Baptism, Eucharist and Ministry (BEM)* and the reports of the Anglican, Lutheran and Reformed dialogues with the Roman Catholic Church. The reception of these international dialogues in Europe is witnessed to in the following agreements, already referred to,[26] which have led to changed relationships: the Meissen Agreement (1988) between the Church of England and the Evangelical Church in Germany, the Porvoo Agreement (1992) between the British and Irish Anglican churches and the Nordic and Baltic Lutheran churches, and the growing communion between Lutheran and Reformed churches in the Leuenberg Agreement (1973) and the continuing theological work done in that context.[27] We understand this present Common Statement as a further example of the reception of theological dialogues in an agreement leading to a changed relationship.

31. The British and Irish Anglican churches and the French Lutheran and Reformed churches are able to record the following agreements in faith. These agreements in faith draw on those in the Meissen Common Statement.[28] They have been reached in the light of the Porvoo Common Statement and the work of the Leuenberg Church Fellowship in a way which shows a high degree of consonance between those texts.

(a) We accept the authority of the canonical Scriptures of the Old and New Testaments. We read the Scriptures liturgically in the course of the Church's year.[29] We believe that through the gospel, God offers eternal life to all humanity, and that the Scriptures contain everything necessary to salvation.[30]

---

[26] Cf. para. 11 above.

[27] Cf. the work on ministry and ecclesiology in *The Church of Jesus Christ*.

[28] Cf. note 12 above.

[29] *Meissen*, para. 15 (i); cf. *Pullach*, paras 17–22.

[30] Cf. *Porvoo*, para. 32 (a) and *Leuenberg*, para. 13.

(b)   We accept the Nicene–Constantinopolitan and Apostles' Creeds
        and confess the basic trinitarian and christological dogmas to which
        these creeds testify. That is, we believe that Jesus of Nazareth is true
        God and true Man, and that God is one God in three persons,
        Father, Son and Holy Spirit.[31] This faith of the Church through the
        ages is borne witness to in the historic formularies of our churches.
        This faith has to be proclaimed afresh in each generation.[32]

(c)   We believe and proclaim the gospel that in Jesus Christ God loves
        and redeems the world. We 'share a common understanding of
        God's justifying grace, i.e. that we are accounted righteous and are
        made righteous before God only by grace through faith because of
        the merits of our Lord and Saviour Jesus Christ, and not on account
        of our works or merits . . . Both our traditions affirm that justifica-
        tion leads and must lead to "good works"; authentic faith issues in
        love'.[33] We receive the Holy Spirit who renews our hearts and
        equips us for and calls us to good works.[34] As justification and sanc-
        tification are aspects of the same divine act, so also living faith and
        love are inseparable in the believer.[35]

(d)   We believe that the Church is constituted and sustained by the
        Triune God through God's saving action in word and sacraments,
        and is not the creation of individual believers. We believe that the
        Church is sent into the world as sign, instrument and foretaste of

---

[31]   *Meissen*, para. 15 (ii); cf. *Pullach*, paras 23–5, *Leuenberg*, para. 12.

[32]   For the Church of England, the Church in Wales and the Church of Ireland, the Thirty-
nine Articles of Religion, *The Book of Common Prayer* and the Ordinal; for the Scottish
Episcopal Church, the *Scottish Prayer Book* and Ordinal. For Lutherans, the symbolic writings
of Lutheranism, particularly the Augsburg Confession and the Small Catechism of Luther.
For the Reformed, the Confessions of the Reformation period. (Cf. the extracts from
ordination rites and declarations of assent appended to this Common Statement.) These
confessional statements were produced in different circumstances and do not play an iden-
tical role in the life of the churches.

[33]   *Meissen*, para. 15 (vi); cf. *Helsinki*, paras 17–21; *Leuenberg*, paras 7, 9 and 10.

[34]   *Porvoo*, para. 32 (c); *All Under One Christ. Statement on the Augsburg Confession by the Roman
Catholic/Lutheran Joint Commission.* Augsburg, 23 February 1980 (published with *Ways to
Community* (Geneva, 1981)), para. 14.

[35]   *Porvoo*, para. 32 (c); *Salvation and the Church. An Agreed Statement by the Anglican–Roman
Catholic International Commission – ARCIC II* (London, 1987), para. 19; cf. *Leuenberg*, para. 10.

the kingdom of God.[36] The Church is a divine reality, holy and transcending present finite reality. At the same time, being also a human institution, it shares all the ambiguity and frailty of the human condition, and is always called to repentance, reform and renewal.[37]

(e)   We celebrate the apostolic faith in liturgical worship. We acknowledge in the liturgy both a celebration of salvation through Christ and a significant factor in forming the *consensus fidelium*.[38] We recognize our common roots in the Western liturgical tradition which give us a similar structure for our eucharistic liturgies, even more manifest as all our churches respond to the common liturgical renewal. We also rejoice in an historical tradition of the reading of Scripture and a resultant biblical spirituality expressed in a number of common prayers, canticles, hymns and metrical psalms. We also note that there is a variety of expressions of worship and sacramental life within each one of our churches as well as between them.

(f)   We believe that through baptism with water in the name of the Father, Son and Holy Spirit, God unites the one baptized with the death and resurrection of Jesus Christ, initiates into the One Holy Catholic and Apostolic Church, and confers the gracious gift of new life in the Spirit.[39] By the power of the Holy Spirit Christ calls the baptized to a new life of faith, to daily repentance and discipleship.[40] Since we in our churches practise and value infant baptism, we also take seriously our catechetical task for the nurture of baptized children to mature commitment to Christ.[41]

---

[36] *Meissen*, para. 15 (vii); cf. *Helsinki*, paras 44–51; *GROU*, paras. 29–34 and *The Church of Jesus Christ*, Chapter I, section 1.

[37] Cf. note 14 above.

[38] *Meissen*, para. 15 (iii); cf. *Helsinki*, para. 31; *GROU*, para. 62; *Baptism, Eucharist and Ministry* (WCC Faith and Order Paper No. 111, 1982) (*BEM*), *Baptism*, para. 17–23, *Eucharist*, paras 27–33, *Ministry*, paras 41–4; *Leuenberg*, para. 28.

[39] Cf. *Porvoo*, para. 32 (g); *Meissen*, para. 15 (iv); *Helsinki*, paras 22–5 and *GROU*, paras 47–61.

[40] Cf. *Leuenberg* para. 14: 'In Baptism Jesus Christ irrevocably receives man, fallen prey to sin and death, into his fellowship of salvation so that he may become a new creature. In the power of his Holy Spirit he calls him into his community and to a new life of faith, to daily repentance and discipleship'; see also para. 11.

[41] *Porvoo*, para. 32 (g).

(g)   We believe that the celebration of the Lord's Supper (the eucharist)
       is the feast of the new covenant instituted by Jesus Christ, in which
       the word of God is proclaimed and in which Christ crucified and
       risen gives his body and blood to the community under the visible
       signs of bread and wine.[42] 'In the action of the Eucharist Christ is
       truly present to share his risen life with us and to unite us with
       himself in his self-offering to the Father, the one full, perfect and
       sufficient sacrifice which he alone can offer and has offered once for
       all.'[43] In this celebration we experience the love of God and the
       forgiveness of sins in Jesus Christ and proclaim his death and
       resurrection until he comes again and brings his kingdom to
       completion.[44] The eucharistic memorial is no mere calling to mind
       of a past event or of its significance, but the Church's effectual
       proclamation of God's mighty acts.[45] Celebrating the eucharist, the
       Church is reconstituted and nourished, strengthened in faith and
       hope, and sent out for witness and service in daily life. Here we
       already have a foretaste of the eternal joy of God's kingdom.[46]

(h)   We believe that all members of the Church are called to participate
       in its apostolic mission. They are therefore given various ministries
       by the Holy Spirit.[47] They are called to offer themselves as 'a living
       sacrifice' and to intercede for the Church and the salvation of the
       world.[48] This is the corporate priesthood of the whole people of
       God, called to ministry and service (1 Peter 2.5).[49] Within the
       community of the Church the ordained ministry exists to serve

---

[42]   Cf. *Meissen*, para. 15 (v) and *Leuenberg*, para. 15. All the participating churches agree that
the liturgical elements of the eucharistic celebration are those listed in *BEM*, E, 27 and also
in note 68 below.

[43]   *GROU*, para. 65.

[44]   *Meissen*, para. 15 (v); cf. *BEM, Eucharist*, para. 1 and *Leuenberg*, para. 16.

[45]   *Porvoo* para. 32 (h); ARCIC, *Final Report, Eucharist*, para. 5; cf. *GROU*, para. 65.

[46]   Cf. *Porvoo*, para. 32 (h) and *Helsinki*, para. 28.

[47]   *Meissen*, para. 15 (viii); cf. *Leuenberg*, para. 13.

[48]   Cf. *Porvoo*, para. 32 (i) and *BEM, Ministry*, para. 17.

[49]   Cf. *Porvoo* 32 (i).

ministry of the whole people of God.[50] For that purpose the ordained ministry of word and sacraments is a gift of God to his Church and may therefore be described as an office of divine institution.[51]

(i)   We believe that a ministry of oversight (*episkope*), exercised in personal, collegial and communal ways,[52] at all levels of the Church's life, is necessary to witness to and safeguard the unity and apostolicity of the Church.[53]

(j)   We share a common hope in the final consummation of the kingdom of God, and believe that in this eschatological perspective we are called to engage now in mission and to work for the furtherance of justice and peace. The obligations of the kingdom are to govern our life in the Church and our concern for the world.[54] In this way the Church witnesses to the new humanity that has its origin and fulfilment in Christ.

32.   This summary witnesses to a high degree of unity in faith and doctrine. Whilst this does not require each tradition to accept every doctrinal formulation characteristic of our distinctive traditions, it does require us to face and overcome the remaining obstacles to still closer communion.

---

[50]   In some traditions, particularly in the Reformed Church of France, the term 'ordained ministry' is not used. They speak of 'recognized ministry'. The theological content of the liturgical act of recognition corresponds to ordination in other churches. Cf. J.-P. Monsarrat, 'The Ministry in the Reformed Church of France', appended to this Common Statement.

[51]   Cf. *Meissen*, para. 15 (viii); cf. *Helsinki*, paras 32–43, *GROU*, paras 73–7 and 91–7; *BEM, Ministry*, paras 41–4 and *The Church of Jesus Christ*, Chapter I, para. 2.5.1.2.

[52]   Cf. J.-P. Monsarrat, 'The Ministry in the Reformed Church of France' and '*Episcope* in the Reformed Church of France' and A. Birmelé, 'The Ministry in the French Lutheran Churches', appended to this Common Statement.

[53]   Cf. *Meissen*, para. 15 (ix) and 16, *BEM, Ministry*, paras 23 and 26; *Pullach*, para. 72 and *GROU*, para. 72.

[54]   *Meissen*, para. 15 (x); cf. *GROU*, paras 18 and 43, *Pullach*, para. 59; *Leuenberg*, para. 9, and *The Church of Jesus Christ*, Chapter I, para. 3.3.4.

VI   The Apostolicity
of the Church and Ministry

33.   All members of the Church are called to participate in its apostolic mission and given various gifts for ministry by the Holy Spirit. Apostolicity belongs to the whole Church. Within the community of the Church the ordained ministry exists to serve the ministry of the whole people of God. We all agree that the life of the Church must be ordered and that all ministry, whether ordained or lay, includes pastoral care and concern for unity at the local and wider than local levels. Further, in all our churches a ministry of oversight is exercised in a personal, collegial and communal (synodical) way.[55]

34.   This ministry of oversight, whether exercised in personal, collegial or communal ways, is a participation in the servant ministry of Christ. In such oversight, authority is characterized by service to the whole Body, even in the context of discipline. *Episkope* after the manner of Christ calls for courageous discerning and self-giving love. It requires openness to the Spirit of truth and the radical values of God's kingdom, against which every exercise of power must be measured. It involves leadership by example. Its purpose is not domination of the people of God but an effective opening-up of the implications of life in Christ for the Church and the world (cf. Mark 10.42-5, John 13.1-17, 2 Corinthians 1.24, Philippians 2.1-11, 1 Peter 5.1-5).

35.   The exercise of the ministry of oversight differs among our churches, however. They give varying degrees of importance to the personal, collegial and communal elements in the overall exercise of oversight. All our churches are churches in change: all are in the process of considering the particular balance between these dimensions. Anglicans, for example, are presently concerned to find the right balance between synodical government and episcopal oversight. The Reformed, because of their experience of history, are concerned that the personal dimension may become so dominant that it is isolated from the community and no longer exercised in relation to the responsibility of the synod.

---

[55]   Cf. footnote 52 above.

36. We all agree that apostolicity belongs to the whole Church. Apostolic succession is the continuous return to the apostolic witness: it is an expression of the permanence, and therefore of the continuity, of Christ's own teaching and mission, in which all the baptized participate.[56] The apostolicity of the Church, as fidelity to the apostolic teaching and mission, is manifested in a *successio fidelium* through the ages.[57] Within the apostolicity of the whole Church is an apostolic succession of the ministry which serves, and is a focus of, the continuity of the Church in its life in Christ and its faithfulness to the words and acts of Jesus transmitted by the apostles.[58] The ordained ministry has a particular responsibility for witnessing to this apostolic tradition and for proclaiming it afresh with authority in every generation.[59]

37. Anglicans believe that the historic episcopate is a sign of the apostolicity of the whole Church. The ordination of a bishop in historic succession (that is, in intended continuity with the apostles themselves) is a sign of God's promise to be with the Church, and also the way the Church communicates its care for continuity in the whole of its faith, life and mission, and renews its intention and determination to manifest the permanent characteristics of the Church of the apostles.[60] Anglicans hold that the full visible unity of the Church includes the historic episcopal succession.

38. Lutherans and Reformed also believe that their ministries are in apostolic succession. In their ordination rites they emphasize the continuity of the Church and its ministry. They can recognize in the historic episcopal succession a sign of the apostolicity of the Church. They do not, however, consider it a necessary condition for full visible unity.

39. Nevertheless, we all agree that the use of the sign of the historic episcopal succession does not by itself guarantee the fidelity of a church to every aspect of the apostolic faith, life and mission. Anglicans increasingly recognize that a continuity in apostolic faith, worship and mission has been preserved in churches which have not retained the historic episcopal succession.[61]

---

[56] Cf. *Porvoo*, para. 39.

[57] Cf. *The Church of Jesus Christ*, Chapter I, para. 2. 3.

[58] *Porvoo*, para. 40; cf. *BEM, Ministry*, para. 34: commentary.

[59] Cf. *Porvoo*, para. 40 and *BEM, Ministry*, para. 35.

[60] Cf. *Porvoo*, para. 50 and paras 47–8.

[61] Cf. *BEM, Ministry*, paras 37 and 53

However, Anglicans commend the use of the sign to signify: God's promise to be with the Church; God's call to fidelity and to unity; and a commission to realize more fully the permanent characteristics of the Church of the apostles.[62]

40. Because of this remaining difference between British and Irish Anglicans and the French Lutheran and Reformed churches our mutual recognition of one another's ministries does not yet result in the full interchangeability of ordained ministers (see para. 27 above and para. 46a (v) below). However, the considerable agreement reached and the changed relationship which would be brought about through this agreement would commit us to work for the visible unity of our churches served by a common ministry.[63]

---

[62] Cf. *Porvoo*, para. 51.

[63] See Chapter VII below.

VII Next Steps

41. We have found a high degree of unity in faith and believe that our churches should express this in a greater degree of visible unity, including the mutual acknowledgement of our churches and our ministries as expressed in the Declaration contained in para. 46 below. The Declaration entails a commitment to deepen and strengthen our communion. We underline three areas of future common work.

A Service and Mission

42. Our churches are called together, particularly in the context of a developing Europe, to make the gospel heard in ways that are understandable and relevant. They are called to be, in the place where God has set them, a credible sign of the kingdom of God. This requires, within the wider ecumenical context, common efforts in witness and service in our societies; joint efforts in facing political, social and ethical issues; shared dialogue with people of other faiths and a fresh exploration together of the relation of majority and minority churches to society and to the State.

B Continuing Theological Work

43. There are a number of issues upon which further convergence is required before our churches are able to give a greater visibility to our unity. These issues are more likely to be resolved within a closer and more committed relationship. We already have a high degree of agreement on the understanding of ministry and ordination.[64] In addition to the issue of historic episcopal succession discussed in Chapter VI, there are some outstanding issues that need discussion.

- The understanding of the one ordained ministry and the different orderings of the ministry within it. For Lutherans and Reformed the one ministry is permanent but the functions within it may be undertaken for a certain period – for example, the ministry of oversight. For Anglicans ordination takes place to the diaconate,

---

[64] Cf. the essays and papers on Ministry appended to this Common Statement.

the presbyterate and the episcopate, three distinctive orders within the one ordained ministry.

- The question of eucharistic presidency.[65]

- The question of the exercising of episcopal oversight or performing episcopal functions by women as well as men.

- The process of formally uniting our ministries.

Closely connected with these questions there are issues of:

- the way authority would be exercised in a visibly united life, including the relation between episcopal-synodical and presbyteral-synodical models of oversight;

- discernment and reception in the decision-making process of the Church;

- the relationship of all our churches to our three Christian world communions.

C   Practical Consequences

44.   This agreement must bear fruit in our everyday lives. We need to discover creative and effective expressions of our new relationship, including:

- regular prayer for and with one another;

- ways of welcoming one another's members into the congregational life of each other's churches;

- especially wherever our churches are in close proximity, taking every opportunity for shared worship and also for joint witness, including common engagement in social, political and economic issues;

- in the case of geographical distance, encouraging appropriate forms of partnership;

- creating opportunities for joint theological education, cultural exchanges, youth camps and post-ordination training, and the provision of suitable library and information technology resources.

---

[65]   See the papers on the Eucharist in our Churches appended to this Common Statement.

45. The suggestions we have made in this chapter are not exhaustive, but they indicate what this Agreement commits us to undertake. The closer relationship between our churches which would be established on the basis of this Common Statement will provide a secure context for facing the outstanding issues. We believe that it is only by continuous conversion to Christ that we shall come nearer to one another in Christ, and by continuous re-formation of our lives that we shall grow nearer to one another and become renewed and enriched in a common life.

VIII   Joint Declaration

46. We recommend that our churches make the following Declaration.

THE REUILLY DECLARATION

We, the Church of the Augsburg Confession of Alsace and Lorraine, the Evangelical–Lutheran Church of France, the Reformed Church of Alsace and Lorraine, the Reformed Church of France, the Church of England, the Church of Ireland, the Scottish Episcopal Church, and the Church in Wales, on the basis of our fundamental agreement in faith, our common understanding of the nature and purpose of the Church, and our convergence on the apostolicity of the Church and the ministry, contained in Chapters II–VI of the *Reuilly Common Statement*, make the following acknowledgements and commitments, which are interrelated.

a   Acknowledgements

(i)   We acknowledge one another's churches as churches belonging to the One, Holy, Catholic and Apostolic Church of Jesus Christ and truly participating in the apostolic mission of the whole people of God.

(ii)   We acknowledge that in all our churches the word of God is authentically preached, and the sacraments of baptism and the eucharist are duly administered.[66]

(iii)   We acknowledge that all our churches share in the common confession of the apostolic faith.

(iv)   We acknowledge that one another's ordained ministries[67] are given by God as instruments of grace for the mission and unity of the Church and for the proclamation of the word and the celebration of the sacraments.

(v)   We acknowledge one another's ordained ministries as possessing not only the inward call of the Spirit but also Christ's commission through the Church, and look forward to the time when the fuller

---

[66]   Cf. *Confessio Augustana*, 7, Article XIX of the Thirty-nine Articles, and *Leuenberg*, para. 2.

[67]   See footnote 50 above.

visible unity of our churches makes possible the interchangeability of ministers.

(vi) We acknowledge that personal, collegial and communal oversight (*episkope*) is embodied and exercised in all our churches in a variety of forms, as a visible sign expressing and serving the Church's unity and continuity in apostolic life, mission and ministry.

b   Commitments

We commit ourselves to share a common life and mission. We will take steps to closer fellowship in as many areas of Christian life and witness as possible, so that all our members together may advance on the way to full visible unity. As the next steps we agree:

(i) to seek appropriate ways to share a common life in mission and service, to pray for and with one another, and to work towards the sharing of spiritual and human resources;

(ii) to welcome one another's members to each other's worship and to receive pastoral ministrations;

(iii) to welcome one another's members into the congregational life of each other's churches;

(iv) to encourage shared worship. When eucharistic worship is judged to be appropriate, it may move beyond eucharistic hospitality for individuals. The participation of ordained ministers would reflect the presence of two or more churches expressing their closer unity in faith and baptism and demonstrate that we are still striving towards making more visible the unity of the One, Holy, Catholic and Apostolic Church. Nevertheless, such participation still falls short of the full interchangeability of ministers. The rite should be that of the church to which the presiding minister belongs, and that minister should say the eucharistic prayer.[68]

---

[68] In such celebrations each church should respect the practices and piety of the others and reflect the emerging ecumenical consensus with regard to the celebration of the eucharist. The celebration will include the prayer of thanksgiving, the words of Christ's institution and the making of the memorial of his sacrifice; the invocation of the Holy Spirit; intercession for the Church and the world and the proclamation of God's kingdom. Ecumenical sensitivity and mutual respect demand that the eucharistic elements are treated reverently after the celebration. The minister who presides at such an ecumenical celebration is an ordained pastor, presbyter or bishop (cf. 'The Lord's Supper' and C. Hill, 'Anglican Eucharistic Practice', appended to this Common Statement). Concelebration is not envisaged.

(v)   to welcome ordained ministers of our churches to serve in each other's churches, in accordance with the discipline of our respective churches, to the extent made possible by our agreement;

(vi)   to continue theological discussions between our churches to work on the outstanding issues hindering fuller communion, whether bilaterally or in a wider European, ecumenical framework;

(vii) to work towards closer relations between ourselves in diaspora situations;

(viii) to encourage ecumenical visits, twinnings and exchanges;

(ix)   to establish a contact group to nurture our growth in communion, to facilitate regular consultation on significant matters, and to co-ordinate the implementation of this agreement.

IX Celebration and Wider Ecumenical Commitment

A Celebration

47. The Declaration will come into force when it is accepted by two participating churches of different traditions according to their own processes. We recommend that our churches express in worship their commitment to share a common life and mission and to continue to strive for the full visible unity of the One Holy Catholic and Apostolic Church.

B Wider Ecumenical Commitment

48. We rejoice in this agreement and see in it a step towards the visible unity which all churches committed to the ecumenical movement seek to manifest. We regard our move to closer communion as part of the pursuit of a wider unity, embracing more and more churches of different traditions. This pursuit will involve the following:

- strengthening the links which each of our churches has with other churches at local, national and international levels;

- deepening relationships within and between our three world communions and supporting efforts towards closer communion between Anglican, Lutheran and Reformed churches in Europe and in those parts of the world where good relations between our church families already exist;

- developing further existing links with other world communions, especially those with whom we have ecumenical dialogue and agreements;

- supporting together our local, national and regional ecumenical councils, the Conference of European Churches and the World Council of Churches.

49. The common inheritance and common calling of our churches, spelt out in this agreement, makes us conscious of our obligation to contribute jointly to the ecumenical efforts of others. At the same time we are aware of our own need to be enriched by the insights and experience of churches

of other traditions and in other parts of the world. Together with them we are ready to be used by God as instruments of his saving and reconciling purpose for all humanity and creation.

MEETINGS OF THE CONVERSATIONS

I   Reuilly Community of Deaconesses, Versailles   7–10 March 1994
        Drafting Group: Strasbourg   8–12 February 1995

II   Emmaus Retreat and Conference Centre, West Wickham
                                    23–28 June 1995
        Drafting Group: Strasbourg   4–6 September 1995

III   Centre Communautaire du Hohrodberg   2–5 June 1996
        Drafting Group: Près de Loirris (Loiret)   4–6 September 1996
        Drafting Group: Strasbourg   18–19 June 1997

IV   Maryvale Pastoral Centre, Bramley, Surrey   9–12 October 1997

PARTICIPANTS

Members

Church of England
The Rt Revd Christopher Hill (Bishop of Stafford)   *Co-Chairman*
The Ven. Martin Draper (Archdeacon of France)
Mrs Elizabeth Fisher
The Revd Canon W J (Barney) Milligan
The Revd Canon Dr Joy Tetley

Church of Ireland
Ms Janet Barcroft

Scottish Episcopal Church
The Revd John Lindsay

Church in Wales

The Rt Revd Huw Jones (Bishop of St Davids)

Church of the Augsburg Confession of Alsace and Lorraine

Pasteur Werner Jurgensen (President of the Lutheran–
Reformed Council)   *Co-Chairman*
Professeur André Birmelé
Pasteur Bertrand Stricker

Evangelical–Lutheran Church of France

Pasteur Marc Chambron

Reformed Church of Alsace and Lorraine

Professeur Isabelle Grellier

Reformed Church of France

Pasteur Michel Bertrand (President of the National Council)
Pasteur Jean-Arnold de Clermont

Consultants

The Revd Canon Richard Marsh (Lambeth Palace)
Pasteur Jean-Pierre Monsarrat
Pasteur Geoffroy de Turckheim (Fédération Protestante de France)

Observers

Père Christian Forster (Roman Catholic Church in France)
The Revd Fleur Houston (United Reformed Church in the United Kingdom)
Präsident Dr Wilhelm Hüffmeier (Leuenberg Church Fellowship)

Staff

Dr Mary Tanner (Church of England)
Dr Colin Podmore (Church of England)

Former Participants

Père Guy Lourmande (Roman Catholic Church in France)
Pasteur Jean Tartier (Fédération Protestante de France)

All papers were sent to: the Evangelical Church in Germany, the Lutheran Council of Great Britain, the Church of Scotland, the Anglican Communion Office, the Lutheran World Federation, the World Alliance of Reformed Churches, the Conference of European Churches, the Faith and Order Commission of the World Council of Churches and the Bishop of Gibraltar in Europe. The aides mémoires of all meetings were also sent to Churches Together in England and the Council of Churches for Britain and Ireland.

THE CHURCHES REPRESENTED IN THE CONVERSATIONS

Anglican Churches

Church of England

Population of England, the Isle of Man and the Channel Islands: 49 million

1996 Christmas communicants: 1,343,000 (3 per cent of over 15s)
1996 electoral rolls: 1,290,400 (c. 3 per cent of over 15s)
1996 usual Sunday attendance: 1,016,000 (2.1 per cent of population)

In 1989 it was estimated that on a given Sunday adult church attendances were divided roughly equally between the Church of England, the Roman Catholic Church and the Free Churches.

2 provinces, 44 dioceses, 12,982 parishes

Primate of All England: The Archbishop of Canterbury
Primate of England: The Archbishop of York

10,004 full-time stipendiary diocesan clergy
perhaps 1,400 non-diocesan clergy
(prison, hospital, Forces, school, college and industrial chaplains; officials)
over 1,900 non-stipendiary clergy
some 6,000 retired clergy holding a licence to officiate

Church of Ireland

Population:	Republic of Ireland	3.5 million
	Northern Ireland	1.6 million

Membership:	Republic of Ireland	95,000 (1981 census)
	Northern Ireland	c. 281,000

2 provinces, 12 dioceses, 466 parishes

Primate of All Ireland:	The Archbishop of Armagh
Primate of Ireland:	The Archbishop of Dublin

518 full-time stipendiary clergy (including bishops)
67 auxiliary clergy
267 retired clergy

Scottish Episcopal Church

1997 membership:	53,000
1997 communicants:	32,000

1 province, 7 dioceses, 321 congregations

Primate:	The Primus (currently the Bishop of Edinburgh)

172 full-time stipendiary clergy
106 non-stipendiary clergy
142 retired clergy

Church in Wales (Yr Eglwys yng Nghymru)

Population of Wales:	2.8 million

1998 Easter communicants:	86,399
1997 electoral rolls:	90,302
1997 usual Sunday attendance:	62,605

1 province, 6 dioceses, 1,142 parishes

Primate: The Archbishop of Wales
              (currently the Bishop of St Asaph)
688 full-time stipendiary diocesan clergy
82 non-stipendiary clergy

French Lutheran and Reformed Churches

1,100,000 (1.8 per cent) of the total population of France are Protestants, between 383,000 and 433,000 of these being Reformed and 240,000 Lutheran.

Reformed Church of France

Membership: 350–400,000
Households contributing financially: 50,000
450 active ministers
482 retired ministers
(1997 figures)

Evangelical–Lutheran Church of France

Membership: c. 40,000

2 ecclesiastical inspectorates, 45 parishes, c. 45 active ministers

Church of the Augsburg Confession of Alsace and Lorraine

Membership: 195,000 (1997)
1997 baptisms 2153, confirmations 1853, marriages 839, burials 2557
7 inspectorates, 40 consistories, 208 parishes

Church leader: The President of the Directory and of the Higher
               Consistory
246 pastors

Reformed Church of Alsace and Lorraine

Membership: 33,000

52 parishes

51 ministers

228,000 (8.8 per cent) of the population of Alsace and Lorraine are members of the Lutheran and Reformed churches.

ESSAYS ON CHURCH, EUCHARIST AND MINISTRY

Contents

An Outline of Our Relationships

Christopher Hill and Jean-Pierre Monsarrat

There have been countless and varied links between the churches of France and the churches of Britain and Ireland, stretching over many centuries from the beginnings of Christianity in both our countries. At the time of the Norman Conquest the ecclesiastical contacts between Northern France and England were intensive. Norman bishops were appointed to English sees, where they began to build the Romanesque and Gothic cathedrals and abbeys of England.

In modern times ecumenical links have been renewed between Anglicans and both French Protestants and the Roman Catholic Church in France. But there is an important and theologically significant chapter in the history of the ecumenical relationships between France and England which is less well known, during the sixteenth and seventeenth centuries. As our churches consider their relationship today, we must not forget the degree of communion we shared in the past.

During the Reformation period and the century which followed there was a real degree of mutual ecclesial recognition between the Church of England and the Reformed Church in France and the Lutheran Church in Strasbourg, in spite of important differences over the form of the ordained ministry.

The early influence of Martin Luther upon reform in England is well known. From Strasbourg Martin Bucer exerted considerable influence upon Archbishop Cranmer's liturgical reforms. Nor can the influence of Jean Calvin on the later stages of the English Reformation be denied. In 1550 Edward VI signed letters patent granting the foundation of the Strangers' Church in London for those 'banished and cast out from their own country for the sake of the Gospel of Christ'. It was the Chapel of St Augustine in Austin Friars in the City of London. Jean à Lasco was appointed by the King as its first superintendent. Many of the refugees spoke Flemish or German and a separate French-speaking congregation was soon established near Spitalfields, which became an important settlement for Huguenot weavers.

During the Roman Catholic restoration in England under Mary Tudor the pastoral and theological links between England and the Continental Reformation churches were intensified as significant numbers of married clergy and lay people went into exile. The Church in Strasbourg, for example, gave hospitality to a number of English Reformers who were eventually to return to episcopal leadership in the Church of England: notably Grindal, Jewel and Sandys. The city also became a centre for English Protestant pamphleteering, the texts being smuggled into England to the considerable annoyance of the Roman Catholic authorities.

With the accession of Elizabeth I the Strangers' Church was re-established with the Bishop of London, Edmund Grindal, as its Superintendent. To this day the appointment of the French Pastor in London is approved by the Crown. After the Elizabethan Settlement a distinctly Anglican approach to the Continental Reformed churches began to emerge. At first Anglicans such as Whitgift, Jewel and Cooper were content to defend episcopacy as a tolerable form of church government over against the criticisms of English Presbyterians. In the writings of Richard Hooker a stronger claim for episcopacy was articulated which was developed further in the next century by the 'Caroline Divines'. This heightened emphasis on episcopacy raised questions for Anglicans about the ministry of the 'non-episcopal' churches of the Continent, not least the French. Nevertheless, Hooker granted that there could be extraordinary exceptions to the episcopal rule he defended against the Puritans in England.

In 1614 James I (James VI of Scotland) sent a message of peace and unity to the Synod of Tonneins. The Synod responded with a resolution proposing a federation of the Church of England and the Reformed and Lutheran churches on the Continent. In 1618 Anglican delegates attended the Reformed Synod of Dort in the Netherlands. While accepting the doctrinal decrees, they objected to its insistence on the parity of ministers as contrary to the Anglican acceptance of episcopacy and the pluriformity of ministries in the New Testament.

With the religious and political confusions of Civil War and Commonwealth in Britain during the seventeenth century, Anglican apologetic for an exclusive doctrine of episcopacy became yet stronger. But most divines continued to refuse to unchurch the Continental Reformed churches. In a famous correspondence with Du Moulin Bishop Lancelot Andrewes spoke of Anglicans not being such 'men of iron' as not to recognize salvation and the Church in the French Reformed Church. That Andrewes spoke representatively is confirmed by the fact that this correspondence was later quoted approvingly by other High Churchmen such as Archbishop Bramhall, and yet again by Archbishop Wake in the eighteenth century.

As to practice, there was some Anglican agreement that the fraternal unity which existed between the English and French Churches permitted the mutual admission of members to communion. Thus Bishop John Cosin admitted Huguenots to communion in Paris during his exile under the Commonwealth. Archbishop Wake similarly administered Holy Communion, baptism and the burial of the dead during his time in Paris as embassy chaplain. Though there was occasional Anglican reserve about communicating at a Reformed eucharist, Bishop Cosin and others were prepared to commend this in cases of pastoral need or, significantly, to demonstrate Anglican unity with the Reformed churches.

The interchangeability of ministers was understandably a more complex issue. There is evidence that non-episcopally ordained clergy were occasionally licensed in the Church of England before 1662. An Elizabethan Act of Parliament of 1570 was commonly regarded as legalizing such ministry. But particular cases are few and far from clear; as time went on the recipients seem to have received such appointments like honorary degrees, for particular pieces of academic work and distinction. Some of the examples are of cathedral appointments to which laymen could also be appointed until 1662. One such was the Du Moulin with whom Bishop Lancelot Andrewes was in correspondence. As well as being a minister of the Reformed Church of France, he also accepted a canonry of Canterbury Cathedral. Whatever the case before 1662, all those who sought to minister in the Church of England after that date were required to have been episcopally ordained or to undergo episcopal ordination. While this requirement was directed against Presbyterians and Independents ordained in England during the Commonwealth period, it inevitably widened the division between the Church of England and the French Protestant churches concerning the ordained ministry. Nevertheless, some Anglicans argued at the time that episcopal ordination did not invalidate a previous ordination. Throughout the sixteenth and seventeenth centuries Anglicans continued to give hospitality to Huguenot refugees, notably the continuous provision for French worship in the Crypt of Canterbury Cathedral, confirmed by Order in Council in 1662 but already long-standing, and an appeal on their behalf by the Bishop of London, Henry Compton, in 1681. The Huguenot refugees, especially after the Revocation of the Edict of Nantes (1685), were to make a material contribution to the cultural and mercantile life of England.

In spite of the important correspondence between Archbishop Wake and Continental Catholic and Protestant theologians, by the middle of the eighteenth century interest in ecumenical contact between England and the Continent was waning. Yet there remained some memory of friendship in the continuing financial support for certain French congregations in England by successive Archbishops of Canterbury and in the licensing of French congregations by successive Bishops of London, which lasted until the time of Blomfield in the nineteenth century. The Evangelical Revival, however, emphasized mission and philanthropy rather than unity. The Tractarian Revival of the nineteenth century did emphasize unity but looked towards Rome and Eastern Orthodoxy. John Keble found the positive attitude of many seventeenth-century High Churchmen to the Continental Lutheran and Reformed churches perplexing. By this time they were regarded by High Churchmen in much the same light as English Free Church dissent.

From the Scottish perspective French political influence at the time of the Reformation was counter-productively influential: French support for the conservative powers-that-be in Scotland caused the Scottish Reformers increasingly to question political opposition to England, which was looked upon as a possible Reformation ally. Thus with the Scottish revolution of 1559 and 1560 the Reformer John Knox reappeared in Scotland from Geneva, in which city he had eventually taken refuge after being involved in an insurrection against the Archbishop of St Andrews in 1547. From 1560 the Auld Alliance with France ceased and with it the end of major French influence in Scotland.

From a French perspective two issues determined French Reformed relationship with the Church of England.

The first was their position in France. The status they had been granted by the Edict of Nantes was constantly weakening. After having lost their political and military guarantees (1629), the actual practice of their faith was gradually threatened. The Protestants rejected the idea that the King was responsible for their plight. They thought they could rely, for their defence, on his faithfulness to the commitments of Henry IV. They wanted to assure him, in return, that they were fully loyal subjects and, when the Revolution broke out in England, that they had nothing to do with those who beheaded Charles I. They condemned, therefore, the Puritan and republican party in England and took sides with those loyal to the English Crown. The second issue was their ecclesiology. Independency and congregationalism were felt as a real threat for the fellowship and unity of the Reformed churches in France. Moreover, some French Reformed churchmen had real sympathies for the Church of England and its bishops. They argued that under the circumstances in which the Reformed churches arose in France, they could not possibly have included in their ministry the historic episcopate, but there was no real theological objection to the episcopal Anglican pattern. In any case, most considered issues related to church polity as not of primary importance. What was decisive for the relationship with the Church of England was for them a fundamental agreement on the gospel and on a common confession of faith. When the Westminster Assembly was meeting and approving the documents that would become the rule for the English-speaking Presbyterian churches, the 1644 National Synod of the Reformed Churches in France denounced the Independents and those that wanted to change the Church of England.

Yet, when the Anglicans took refuge in Paris at the death of Charles I, the French Reformed realized that there was reluctance among some Anglicans to join with their Reformed brethren for Holy Communion. Up to the Revocation (1685) and in England afterwards French churchmen persistently argued in favour of communion between the Reformed churches of France and the Church of England.

Mention has already been made of the Du Moulin family. The father, a minister of the Reformed Church, was called upon by King James to reply to Cardinal Du Perron who wrote against the King and the Church of England. Thus Du Moulin championed the English Reformation against the Roman criticisms. It was for this that he was made a canon of Canterbury. He made no secret of his thinking that episcopacy had many merits. His son Peter became a priest of the Church of England; in 1664 he published an English translation of the book his father had written in

1627 to defend Anglicanism. In introducing the book, he explained at length why the Reformed churches in France could not be blamed for lacking bishops. His brother Louis also settled in England but he became a Dissenter. The third son remained in France as a minister of the Reformed Church quite content with its presbyteral-synodical government.

From 1685 onwards, the Reformed churches were outlawed in France. Those that remained Protestants at heart were too busy trying to rebuild their church underground to give thought to matters such as their relationship with the Church of England. The issue only concerned those who had taken refuge in the British Isles, and their links with their home church and country grew weak and disappeared in a matter of one or two generations.

After the turmoil of the French Revolution, Napoleon, by an Act of 1802, gave the Reformed and the Lutherans legal recognition alongside the Roman Catholics and brought their churches under the protection and control of the State. Much was given, but one essential thing was withheld: the authority to convene a National Synod. In a century during which the churches underwent disruptive influences of all kinds, they were deprived of the normal means of settling conflicts. Nor could the churches consider, at the national level, their relationships with other churches.

Yet Protestants in France were deeply involved in ventures with Protestants of other lands, in particular from the British Isles. As their involvement was often due to the influence of the Evangelical Revival, they shared the undertakings of the evangelical wing of the British churches, regardless of denomination. The Paris Mission, set up in 1822, was a close partner, all through the century, of the London City Missionary Society, and wary about the Society for the Propagation of the Gospel, which was regarded as 'ritualistic'.

In a completely different area of the life of the Church, it must be mentioned that some were attracted by the liturgical wealth of the Anglican tradition: Eugène Bersier, for instance, a Reformed minister who had spent some time in the United States of America with the Episcopal Church, made an important contribution to the growth of the liturgical awareness of the French Reformed Church.

Mention must also be made of the name of Tommy Fallot (1839–1904), regarded as the founder of the Christian social movement. He was also profoundly concerned with the future of the Church. Marc Boegner, his nephew and disciple, quotes him: 'The Church will be catholic or shall not be; the Christian shall be Protestant or will disappear . . . I hereafter consider myself as an Evangelical Catholic . . .' It is interesting that he should thus reclaim the use of the adjective 'Catholic' which had become completely synonymous with 'Roman Catholic' for the average Protestant (and still largely remains so).

The French Protestant churches recovered their full freedom in 1905. But it is thanks to the Ecumenical Movement, in which the Reformed and Lutheran churches took full part from the start, that they have become involved, once again, in bi- and multilateral relations with other churches and amongst them the Anglican churches. So though our churches gradually lost the contact established at the Reformation and maintained throughout the seventeenth and early eighteenth centuries, in the twentieth century the Ecumenical Movement has brought our churches closer together again. From 1956 to 1970 there took place six unofficial Theological Conferences between members of the Church of England and the French Reformed Church. At the last there was a French Lutheran observer. These conferences discussed Christian worship, prayer and devotion, Christian initiation, the ministry, intercommunion and the doctrine of the Church.

PROFILES OF OUR CHURCHES

The Anglican Communion

Colin Podmore and Christopher Hill

The Anglican Communion has no written overall church order or canons, but is united by four main instruments of unity or 'bonds of communion'. The four Anglican churches represented in these conversations are constituent members. The Church of England as such does not today have a determinative role within the Communion.

The Lambeth Conference

The Lambeth Conference is a gathering of bishops whose churches are in communion with the See of Canterbury. It meets every ten years at the invitation and under the presidency of the Archbishop of Canterbury. Although the Conference's resolutions have no canonical status and are not binding on the member churches, they do possess a significant degree of moral authority by virtue of the bishops being gathered together. The first Lambeth Conference was held in 1867, and the thirteenth was held in Canterbury in 1998.

The Anglican Consultative Council

The Anglican Consultative Council, established in 1969, is an international assembly of the Anglican Communion, consisting of bishops, clergy and lay people from each of the member churches. It meets every two or three years. As its name suggests, it is a consultative body, with no legislative powers.

The Primates' Meeting

Since 1979 a meeting of Anglican primates has been held every two or three years. Each member church of the Anglican Communion is represented by its senior primate, archbishop or presiding bishop. The Primates' Meeting facilitates consultation, but cannot take binding decisions.

The Anglican Communion Office

These bodies and the Anglican Communion as a whole are serviced by a permanent secretariat led by the Secretary General of the Anglican Communion. The Anglican Communion Office is in London.

Member Churches

The Anglican Communion includes 32 autonomous member churches, consisting of one or more Provinces. The four United Churches (South and North India, Pakistan and Bangladesh) which incorporate former Anglican dioceses are also members, as are five extra-provincial dioceses (three of which have the Archbishop of Canterbury as their Metropolitan).

Each of the churches has its own constitution. All have an episcopal and synodical polity, but it is impossible to generalize more than this. For example, the senior bishop of some churches is merely a *primus inter pares,* whereas other Anglican churches (such as the Church of England) have a primate or primates with metropolitical jurisdiction throughout their respective provinces.

Churches in Communion

In addition to the member churches of the Anglican Communion, there are other churches which are in communion with the See of Canterbury. These include, for example, the Old Catholic churches and those Nordic and Baltic Lutheran churches which have approved the Porvoo Declaration.

The Church of England

Colin Podmore

When Christianity came to Britain is not known, although some evidence suggests a Christian presence by about 200. In 314 the Church was sufficiently well established to be represented by the Bishops of London, York and a third British see at the Council of Arles. In the fifth century, however, southern and eastern Britain was invaded by pagan Angles, Saxons and Jutes. The Church continued in Wales, and in the sixth century Cornwall was evangelized from there and from Ireland. It was from Ireland, too, that St Columba (c. 521–97) travelled to found Iona, from whence St Aidan (d. 651) led the mission which was to re-establish the Church in Northumbria. He was consecrated bishop in 635 and established his see on Lindisfarne. Meanwhile, in 597, St Augustine (d. c. 604) had landed in Kent at the head of a mission sent by the Pope, St Gregory the Great, to re-evangelize England.[1]

Although St Augustine's mission was thus by no means the only source of English Christianity, the *Ecclesia Anglicana* (Anglican or English Church) can be said to stem chiefly from it. Seventy years after Augustine's arrival, however, the English Church was in a state of some disorder. Theodore of Tarsus (c. 602–90) was sent from Rome to become Archbishop of Canterbury, arriving in 669. Having supplied bishops for the many vacant sees, he called a council which met at Hertford in 672. This council involved the whole English Church, and agreed a set of canons which could be described as its founding charter.[2] Bede described Theodore as 'the first of the archbishops whom the whole English Church consented to obey'. Perhaps Theodore's most lasting achievement was the creation of the English diocesan system. Dividing the existing large dioceses, most of which covered the area of one of the English kingdoms, he established

---

[1]   For a recent survey of the history of episcopacy in the Church of England, see C. Hill, 'Episcopacy in our Churches: England' in *Together in Mission and Ministry. The Porvoo Common Statement with Essays on Church and Ministry in Northern Europe* (GS 1083, London, 1993), pp.125–36.

[2]   P. Wormald, 'The Venerable Bede and the "Church of the English"' in D.G. Rowell (ed.), *The English Religious Tradition and the Genius of Anglicanism* (Wantage, 1992), p.17.

diocesan boundaries which are still recognizable today. It is not too much to claim that Theodore was the English Church's second founder.

The division of the English Church into two provinces dates from 735, when Pope Gregory III approved the raising of the bishopric of York to an archbishopric. Lanfranc (c.1042–89), who was Archbishop of Canterbury from 1070, asserted the supremacy of Canterbury over York, but this was not finally settled until 1353, when it was accepted that the Archbishop of Canterbury should be styled Primate of All England and the Archbishop of York Primate of England. By the beginning of the fifteenth century the Convocations of Canterbury and York, provincial synods each consisting of an upper house of bishops and a lower house of clergy, had taken shape.

The English Reformation

The series of events which are collectively described as 'the English Reformation' took place over 30 years, in several distinct phases, beginning with the meeting of the Reformation Parliament in 1529 and culminating in the 'Elizabethan Settlement' of 1559. What may (anachronistically) be termed 'Anglicanism', as a distinctive body of beliefs, was, however, to reach maturity only in the following century.

The first phase, under Henry VIII, was essentially political. On 15 May 1532 the Convocation of Canterbury agreed the Submission of the Clergy, whereby the Convocations could only meet if summoned by royal writ and could make no canons without royal licence. Canon law was subordinated to the common and statute law of England. Acts of Parliament abolished payments and appeals from England to Rome, and the Pope's legal rights in England were divided between the Crown and the Archbishops. The 1534 Act of Supremacy declared that the King was 'the only supreme head in earth of the Church of England'. Between 1536 and 1540 the monastic houses of England were dissolved, a development which arguably owed more to the Crown's need for money and the financial aspirations of its supporters than to any strictly theological or ecclesiastical motives. Thus, in the reign of Henry VIII the English Church was effectively separated and nationalized. The King replaced the Pope and seized a considerable proportion of the Church's wealth, but with the notable exception of the monastic life, its internal system remained intact.

An English Bible was ordered to be placed in every parish church (1538) and an English Litany introduced (1544), but otherwise little official doctrinal or liturgical change occurred. Henry VIII died in 1547, over seventeen years after the meeting of the Reformation Parliament, never having heard the Mass other than in Latin.

The second phase of the English Reformation occurred in the brief but turbulent reign of Edward VI (1547–53). Now there was doctrinal change, but, significantly, it was expressed first and foremost in liturgical change, centrally in the Prayer Books of 1549 and 1552, of which the Archbishop of Canterbury, Thomas Cranmer, was the chief author. The Church of England would continue to express its beliefs chiefly in its liturgy. Cranmer's liturgies built on the medieval liturgical tradition, echoing its prayers. In this they resembled those of German Lutheranism, another important influence, and differed from the essentially non-liturgical worship of the Swiss Reformed churches. Doctrinally, however, the 1552 Prayer Book showed Reformed influence, as did the Forty-two Articles which followed in 1553. One important difference was that the English Ordinal consciously retained the term 'priest' and provided for the continuation of the three orders of bishop, priest and deacon inherited from the primitive Church. In this second phase of the Reformation, liturgy and doctrine had been changed, but again the historic structure and order of the Church remained intact.

In the even briefer reign of Mary (1553–8), most of the changes of her father and brother were undone. Reginald Pole, as papal legate, was invited to reconcile England to the Holy See, and on 30 November 1555 five hundred Members of Parliament knelt to receive his absolution, as did the Convocation of Canterbury six days later. The Papal Supremacy and the Latin Mass were restored. In 1556 Cardinal Pole succeeded Cranmer as Archbishop of Canterbury, but he was to be the last archbishop who was in communion with the See of Rome. He and his Queen both died on 17 November 1558.

By the 1559 Act of Supremacy Elizabeth I accepted the amended title 'Supreme Governor of the Church of England'. The 1559 Act of Uniformity reintroduced the 1552 *Book of Common Prayer*, slightly amended in a conservative direction. Of the bishops, only those of Llandaff and Sodor and Man remained in office. Matthew Parker was appointed Archbishop of Canterbury and consecrated in Lambeth Palace

Chapel on 17 December 1559. None of Mary's bishops being willing to act, the consecration was performed by three former diocesan bishops and a suffragan. Again, liturgy preceded doctrinal definition. In 1562–3 the Forty-two Articles were amended and reduced in number, and as the Thirty-nine Articles they reached their final form in 1570. The Articles can be characterized as moderately Reformed, but were so framed as to comprehend as many as possible within the Church of England. The 1604 Canons of the Church of England furnished the Church with a code of canon law, but did not repeal the medieval canon law in areas which they did not address.

The English Reformation was marked not by innovation but by rejection of the innovations of Rome. Its intention was to get back to the pure faith and order of the early or 'primitive' Church. This position was defended against Roman Catholic criticism on the one hand by Bishop John Jewel (1522–71) in his *Apology* (1562) and against Puritan insistence that the Church of England was not fully reformed by Richard Hooker (c. 1554–1600). In the seventeenth century this concern led to a flowering of patristic scholarship on the part of Anglican divines which was unrivalled in any other church, and devotion to the ideal of the primitive Church was to persist into the middle years of the eighteenth century and beyond.[3]

Abolition and Restoration

First, however, this developing 'Anglicanism' was driven underground or into exile by the victory of Parliament over Charles I in the Civil War (1642–6). In 1645 Archbishop William Laud and then in 1649 the King himself were executed. During this radical break in the Church of England's history, its structure, episcopal ministry and liturgy were abolished. Only its buildings remained, and they were despoiled. From as early as 1651 concern grew amongst loyal churchmen that the Church of England's episcopal succession might die out, and indeed by the end of 1659 all but nine of its 27 sees were vacant. The exiled King Charles II repeatedly attempted to persuade the survivors to consecrate new bishops, but they were too fearful to act on his orders within England, while age and infirmity held them back from travelling to the Continent. Had the

---

[3]   See E. Duffy, 'Primitive Christianity Revived; Religious Renewal in Augustan England', *Studies in Church History*, xiv (1977), 287–300.

Interregnum lasted even just ten years longer, the Anglican episcopal succession would probably have been extinguished.

In fact, after the Restoration of the Monarchy in 1660, the episcopally ordered Church of England was restored also. Under the 1662 Act of Uniformity, some 1,900 clergy who were not episcopally ordained or who refused to use the revised *Book of Common Prayer* were ejected. After the 'Glorious Revolution' (1689) toleration was preferred to comprehension, and it was tacitly accepted that there would continue to be substantial bodies of Christians who dissented from the Church of England and maintained a separate religious life. The Church of England was now settled in its identity. In the eighteenth century, the Church of England's failure to retain John Wesley's Methodism within its structures increased the proportion of English Christians who did not belong to it, as did large-scale (Roman Catholic) Irish immigration in the following century.

The Nineteenth and Twentieth Centuries

During the nineteenth century a number of developments and movements greatly affected the Church of England's character. From the 1830s, ecclesiastical reforms began to modernize the Church's organization and redistribute its revenues, while Evangelicals, Liberals and Catholics occupied increasingly distinctive positions. Each of these streams has its successors today, and in addition to this, practices and insights which were originally distinctive to each of them can now be found much more widely within the Church of England. Visually (in the conduct of worship, liturgical dress, church furnishings, etc.) and in terms of its understanding of its own identity, the image which the Church of England overall has presented in the second half of the twentieth century owes more to the Anglo-Catholic Oxford Movement and its successors than to either of the other streams. In these respects, the Church of England as a whole would have been very different had it not been for the Oxford Movement. *The Tracts for the Times* (1833–41), whose main authors were John Henry Newman, John Keble and Edward Bouverie Pusey, stressed the Church of England's identity as part of the Catholic Church and the apostolic authority of its bishops, derived from the historic, apostolic succession. Significantly, one of the Tractarians' chief projects was the 83-volume *Library of Anglo-Catholic Theology* (1841–63), an edition of the works of the most notable seventeenth-century Anglican divines. This was the heritage which the Tractarians revived and on which they built, and its influence can be seen in the fact that the other great Tractarian publishing project was a *Library of the Fathers* (translations of the major patristic writings). As time went on, the Oxford Movement's emphasis on sacramental worship combined with other Victorian influences to revive Catholic ritual, architecture and church furnishing and enrich the Church of England's worship liturgically and musically. It also resulted in the revival of religious orders in the Church of England.

The twentieth century has seen a gradual increase in the practical independence of the Church from the State. In 1919 the Church Assembly, consisting of the Convocations and a House of Laity, was established to process Church legislation, which Parliament would approve or reject but not amend. In 1970 a new General Synod, inheriting most of the powers of the Convocations (which continued to exist) and all those of the Church Assembly, was inaugurated. By the Worship and Doctrine Measure 1974 the General Synod received powers to authorize new and alternative services without Parliamentary approval. Under a protocol of 1977, a Church body, the Crown Appointments Commission, was given a decisive role in the appointment of diocesan bishops. A new code of canon law was promulged by the Convocations between 1964 and 1969, replacing the Canons of 1604, and in *The Alternative Service Book* (1980) the Church gained a definitive modern liturgy to complement the historic liturgy of *The Book of Common Prayer.*

In February 1994 the General Synod promulged a canon providing for the ordination of women to the priesthood. This was seen by the majority as a legitimate development of the ordained ministry, but by a substantial minority as effecting a major change in the Church of England's identity and self-understanding as part of the Catholic Church. Provision was made by Act of Synod for the continuing diversity of opinion in the Church of England in this matter.

The Church of England's understanding of its identity today is set out in the Preface to the Declaration of Assent.[4]

This essay is reprinted from *Anglican–Moravian Conversations: The Fetter Lane Common Statement with Essays in Moravian and Anglican History* (CCU Occasional Paper No. 5, 1996).

---

[4] See p. 97 below.

The Church of Ireland

Kenneth Milne

The Church of Ireland is Anglican and is the Protestant episcopal church in Ireland. At the time of the Reformation, in the mid-sixteenth century, only parts of Ireland were effectively under English control. It was in those areas (especially the region around Dublin called the Pale and most other large towns) that Henry VIII's religious changes were imposed. Imposed, it must be said, on a largely complaisant Irish hierarchy who had, from medieval times, been accustomed to accepting a great deal of royal control over church matters. Furthermore the Reformation under Henry, though radical in the matter of breaking with the papacy and in the suppression of the monasteries, was not so radical in matters of doctrine and worship, and this made it easier for bishops to accept. The Church of Ireland was the established church and remained so for the best part of 350 years, though it was never the church of a majority of the people of Ireland. Its numbers grew from the original nucleus of the people of the Pale and the towns (especially public servants and the professional classes), as successive generations of English settlers and officials came into the country in the succeeding centuries. At the present time the number of Church of Ireland members on the entire island is about 360,000. Something like a quarter of these live in the Republic, where they account for a little more than 3 per cent of the population of the state.

The Irish establishment, both political and religious, suffered severe shocks in the seventeenth century from both Puritans and Jacobites, and a severe code of penal laws, mainly against Roman Catholics but also depriving Protestant dissenters of political power, copper-fastened the privileged position of the Church of Ireland in religious matters and of the Protestant ascendancy landlord class in matters political. These laws provided inducements for some Roman Catholics and Dissenters to 'conform' to the Church of Ireland, as did certain evangelical missions to various parts of the country, particularly during the 'second reformation' of the early decades of the nineteenth century. When Gladstone forced disestablishment on the Church of Ireland in 1870, it still remained very much the church of the influential classes until the greater part of Ireland achieved independence in the 1920s. The Church of Ireland possesses most of the ancient Irish cathedrals, since by and large their chapters (and especially in the towns, many of the more influential members of the population), however reluctantly, accepted the Reformation changes.

The Church of Ireland, as a minority church long dependent on the British connection for its privileged position, inevitably bred in its people (with some remarkable exceptions such as Charles Stewart Parnell and Douglas Hyde) a strong attachment to the English crown. Until recent generations, most Church of Ireland people belonged to the unionist (with a small 'u') tradition, and, to use a current term, were in many instances alienated from the Irish Free State, which was avowedly Gaelic in its cultural policies, and (less avowedly) Roman Catholic in its social policy. By degree, however, thanks in no small measure to a sensitivity (on most issues) shown by the State to the Protestant minority, more recent generations of Irish Anglicans have easily identified with the independent state, being perhaps encouraged in this by the fact that while Protestant nationalists and republicans were a minority within a minority, they have a place in the Irish republican tradition.

Political differences between Protestants and Roman Catholics have largely disappeared. More lasting have been different social mores that grew out of religious practice. A good example of these is the attitude, not only of members of the Church of Ireland, but of Protestants in general, to Sunday observance. It has not been customary, at least until very recent times, for Protestants to attend cinemas or play team games on Sundays. Of course, there have always been exceptions. But by and large Protestants have observed Sunday in a more subdued way than have their Roman Catholic neighbours. For this reason (among others) the Protestant community in an area has tended not to engage in Sunday games, nor to organize parish functions on Sundays. Such attitudes have been understood and respected by the rest of the community, but have tended to result in a separateness that could sometimes be construed as keeping one's distance. Younger generations are less inclined to maintain this distinction.

The Church of Ireland is a member church of the Anglican Communion, and as such it shares the doctrine and church order of those churches in communion with the See of Canterbury. Its teaching is defined as being that of Scripture, the primitive Church and reason explicitly linked together, and its worship is according to set liturgical forms. By comparison with, say, the Church of England or the Episcopal Church in the United States, Church of Ireland services have been very plain and conventional. This was partly due to a strict set of regulations introduced at disestablishment when, self-governing for the first time, the Church of Ireland reacted (perhaps overreacted) against both the prevailing ethos of the Roman Catholic church that surrounded it and the growth of Anglo-Catholic attitudes and practices in England.

Many of the issues that were the cause of strenuous debate a hundred years ago have ceased to be contentious. Crosses and lighted candles are no longer prohibited on altars (though the word 'altar' would not be in common Church of Ireland usage). Yet though somewhat austere in her forms of worship, the Church of Ireland is impeccably Anglican in theology, blending 'Catholic' and 'Protestant' traditions. With the introduction of *The Alternative Service Book* in 1984, a much greater flexibility in the ordering of services is now possible. New forms of service provide striking resemblances to the forms of worship used in other churches, not only within Anglicanism, and so contribute to an ecumenical spirit. Anglican yet Irish, the Church of Ireland has a profound feeling for the Celtic roots of Irish Christianity; Patrick, Brigid and Colmcille have a place in the liturgical calendar. Prayers and hymns from ancient Irish sources are popular with congregations. And from a Church of Ireland background have come lovers of the Irish language, before and since Douglas Hyde, who have been dedicated to its revival. Yeats, O'Casey, Lady Gregory, Synge and Beckett helped to form the intellectual identity of modern Ireland, and artists of the calibre of Mainie Jellett and Oisin Kelly in glass and stone have made distinctive contributions to Irish spirituality.

As in worship, so also in doctrine, the Church of Ireland is conservative. Yet by comparison with the other Irish churches, not particularly so. Indeed, in matters of moral theology, and in its contribution to public debate on divorce and contraception (both of which have now been legislated for in the Republic), the Church of Ireland has advanced an alternative Christian view. The Church of Ireland shares in the developing theology that has been a mark of the Anglican approach of recent years, and however cautiously, wishes to contribute to the effort being made by a comparatively new state, the Irish Republic, to formulate its moral attitudes.

The Church of Ireland has a long tradition of overseas work, which continues and which is complemented by the Bishops' Appeal for World

Development and support for under-developed and developing countries. Changed times have also brought significant initiatives in youth work, the Church of Ireland Youth Council having a very highly organized administration served by full-time staff, the work in the Republic being supported by funds provided by Church and State. Gradually the importance of a good understanding of the role of the mass media in our society has been appreciated, as also has the importance of ecumenical activity in media matters, north and south.

The Church of Ireland owns a considerable amount of diocesan and parish property throughout the island. This is usually vested in the Representative Church Body, which also holds most of those church funds that are earmarked for clergy salaries and pensions. The offices of the Representative Church Body are in Dublin, as are the National Cathedral (St Patrick's) and the Church of Ireland Theological College. Dublin is where the General Synod usually meets, and there are historical reasons why this should be so, for Dublin was the historical seat of government for the island and the administration of the Established Church was naturally located there. But even in the 1990s, when three-quarters of the Church of Ireland population live in Northern Ireland, Dublin's focal position is not seriously challenged. This is no doubt very largely because of tradition. But it is also because the all-Ireland nature of the Church of Ireland is a reality, and Dublin is unquestionably the communications centre of Ireland.

The members of the Church who live in the Republic are influential in the life and work of the Church. They share some perspectives with their fellow churchmen in the north, though many of them hold different views, particularly in political matters. It was because of these varied viewpoints of Church of Ireland members that it was decided to accept an invitation to give evidence, written and oral, to the Forum for Peace and Reconciliation established by the Irish Government, and, incidentally, presided over by a judge who is a member of the General Synod of the Church of Ireland. In this way, and in meeting with representatives of political parties of all complexions, north and south, the Church of Ireland attempts to show readiness to share in the search for a political solution to Ireland's major problems. The Church of Ireland's past history and present situation, part of a minority in the Republic and part of a majority in the North, make her peculiarly suited to doing so.

The Scottish Episcopal Church

John Lindsay

It is not for glory, riches or honours that we fight; it is for liberty alone, the liberty which no good man relinquishes but with his life.

The words of the Declaration of Arbroath (1320) record the determination of the Scottish nation to resist all interference by Pope John XXII, or anyone else, in its internal affairs. The Scots' independence of spirit may also be explained in the particular relationship that developed between landowner and labourer following the decline in population due to the Black Death. By the middle of the fourteenth century serfdom was virtually unknown north of the border, replaced by the mutual trust and devotion as between tenant and laird. There was much less tension between various ranks of society than was experienced in England or Germany.

Notwithstanding attempts at reform of the Church by John Hamilton, Archbishop of St Andrews, by the sixteenth century monastic and parochial life was in a state of decay. The Scottish Church was fertile ground for the reforming influences that had begun flooding in from the Continent. Merchants brought Lutheran books into Scottish east coast ports from the Low Countries and Scandinavia and their teachings spread rapidly. Martyrdoms and riots occurred in various places and by 1560 under the leadership of John Knox, a Genevan Calvinist, the old order was overthrown.

The fact that the Scottish Reformation occurred later than on the Continent may account for the different models of reform advocated in Scotland. Knox himself was not opposed to the reformed ideal of the 'godly bishop' and it has been shown that his 'superintendents' could be viewed as a rationalized form of episcopacy. The novelty in the Scottish situation was that the partisans of both models, Presbyterian and Episcopalian, stayed together in one church for over a century, albeit squabbling along the way under pressure from whatever monarch was in power.

What battles there were between warring factions within the Church no doubt resulted in still-remembered martyrdoms, though mercifully there were fewer than in England or the Continent. For 130 years Lutheran and Calvinist influences intertwined in an ever-changing and developing Reformed Church of Scotland, now one and now the other being dominant.

The prevailing group within Scotland, however, advocated a staunchly Presbyterian polity, under the guidance of Andrew Melville and other seventeenth-century divines. Thus, when in 1689 William of Orange came to the throne of the then United Kingdom the Claim of Right included among its grievances the fact that the Crown had repeatedly used the Estate of Bishops to control the country. And since the Scottish Bishops, like some of their fellow non-jurors in England, refused to give their oath of allegiance on the grounds that their oath to King James could not be revoked, William turned to the Presbyterian party and by Act of Parliament declared the Church of Scotland to be Presbyterian.

Thus the Scottish Episcopal Church came into being as a distinct and separate minority, repressed, as a pro-French fifth column, by the British Government using its troops for the purpose, and evicted from its parish churches, though in many remote areas this took some time to achieve. The offer of a measure of religious tolerance, provided worship was conducted by Church of England clergy using the English Prayer Book, was accepted by chapels which thus 'qualified'. However, the Scottish bishops joined the Jacobite cause with the result that after the risings of 1715 and 1745 the Episcopal Church, with the exception of those 'qual-ified chapels', was outlawed and all but disappeared until the partial repeal of the Penal Laws in 1792. During this period Scottish Episcopalians learned to value the freedom to elect their own bishops and to exercise their financial and other responsibilities without support or interference from either Crown or State.

No history of the Scottish Episcopal Church can fail to mention the consecration, during those difficult years, of Dr Samuel Seabury of Connecticut so that American Episcopalians could have their own bishops and no longer continue under the Bishop of London. The consecration in Aberdeen on 14 November 1784 is not only an event of some pride for Scottish Episcopalians but also a defining moment for the whole Anglican Communion.

It was not until after the death of Bonnie Prince Charlie that the Scottish Episcopal Church could act to remove the suspicion of disloyalty to the Protestant Succession. The Jacobite movement had lost the object of its devotion and, following the Act of Toleration 1792, Scottish Episcopalians affirmed their agreement in doctrine with the Church of England. A number of the 'qualified chapels' were reconciled, accepting the jurisdiction of the Scottish bishops, revisions of a distinctively Scottish Prayer Book were undertaken, canon law was codified and the work of mission was extended into new centres of population. The nineteenth century saw the Episcopal Church begin a period of growth and development with an ambitious programme of church building.

Both the Evangelical Revival and the Tractarian Movement had their effect, the latter especially reinforcing the Episcopal Church's conviction that it was the guardian of the true faith in Scotland. And the Church's missionary efforts were directed at both those with no church links, the working classes and immigrant labour force, and also members of other churches. This activity met with considerable success and the Church grew in numbers and resources. A Theological College was established and some notable scholars, especially in the fields of liturgy and history, enriched the Church's life.

The process of church expansion continued well into the twentieth century, although striking changes have been seen since the end of World War II. Synodical government has developed rapidly, liturgies have been revised and indeed rewritten, the ministry of women has been acknowledged and relationships with other churches have grown in depth and warmth. At the same time, along with other churches, questions and challenges about role and influence in the Scotland of today are being addressed.

The paramount importance of sharing the faith with those who know little or nothing of it is beginning to be recognized. The way in which this sharing is done differs from congregation to congregation, but at its heart lies a distinctive liturgical tradition and the need to listen to and to be in dialogue with others. Being free from the responsibilities incumbent on the Established Church, the Scottish Episcopal Church is perhaps freer to undertake new initiatives with a distinctively attractive *joie de vivre*.

The Church in Wales

Huw Jones

Wales is the westernmost part of mainland Britain, a highland country, divided by its geography into a number of distinct regions. The word 'Wales' and 'Welsh' are derived from the ancient Germanic word *wealas* 'foreigner', applied by the incoming Anglo-Saxons to the native British who inhabited the western part of Britain. The Welsh call themselves *Cymry* – 'fellow-countrymen' – and their land *Cymru*. They are the descendants of the original Celtic peoples who occupied much of Britain before and after the Roman conquest and who originally migrated from Gaul. Hence the French description – *Pays de Galles* and *Gallois*. In describing the Christian history of Wales we can discern four main periods.

The Early Period up to 1100

The beginnings of British Christianity are not recorded; it was probably brought into Britain by soldiers, traders and travelling craftsmen in the time of the Roman occupation. By the year 206 Britain had produced its first martyrs, Alban at St Albans and Julius and Aaron at Caerleon in south-east Wales. By 314 there were three British bishops present at the Council of Arles. The Roman army left Britain towards the end of the fourth century and in the next century much of England was occupied by successive waves of invaders from Europe – Saxons, Angles and Jutes. They were pagans and Christianity disappeared from the areas they conquered.

In the west the Church remained and gradually grew in the Celtic lands of Wales, Scotland, Cornwall, Ireland and Britanny. This was the age of the saints, the age of the missionaries, who preached the gospel and built up Christian communities. They were deeply influenced by the eremitical and monastic movement which had originated in the East and had come to Britain via Gaul. The most prominent of these in Wales were Cadog, Teilo, Padarn, who worked in the south and west, Beuno in the north and above all David or Dewi in the south-west, who was in medieval times to

73

become the patron saint of Wales. They worked through communities, and the major churches associated with them became 'mother' churches, centres of missionary and scholarly activity, from which the surrounding area was evangelized. Their work is commemorated not only in the lives of the saints, which were written centuries later, but also in the hundreds of Welsh place names with the prefix 'llan' or church, followed by the name of its founder or its patron saint. The Church, in common with that of the rest of Europe, would have been episcopally led, but dioceses in those centuries would have been based more on tribal rather than territorial divisions, and the bishop would have been closely associated with the local prince or chieftain.

The Medieval Church

The Norman conquest of Wales was a piecemeal affair and was not completed until 1284 when the last of the many independent princedoms was subjugated. One aspect of this gradual conquest was a determination to control the Welsh Church and bring it under the sovereignty of the Crown and the Archbishop of Canterbury. The four territorial dioceses of Bangor, St Davids, Llandaff and St Asaph came into existence, and a parish structure was gradually set up. The kings, and Henry I in particular, attempted to ensure that all bishops were political nominees favourable to Norman rule, if not Norman themselves. All bishops were forced to owe obedience to the Archbishop of Canterbury. The new bishops spared no effort to overhaul the organization of the Church and to eradicate surviving Celtic practices, such as the marriage of the clergy. Benedictine monasteries were set up to replace the Welsh houses and revenues were diverted to mother houses in England or France. The later Cistercian foundations proved to be more congenial to the Welsh. The literature of the later middle ages suggests that the Church was held in high regard and that devotional practices were widespread.

The Modern Period from 1536 to 1920

Two factors which have shaped modern Welsh history need to be noted. First, under the Tudors, Wales was united to, or more accurately absorbed into, England. The language was given no official status and there were no national institutions. Secondly, the Industrial Revolution had a profound effect on much of south Wales and north-east Wales from 1780 onwards. The population greatly increased and the large bulk of the population became town dwellers. The mass immigration from parts of England and Ireland led to the Welsh language becoming a minority language. In 1871 66 per cent of the population was Welsh-speaking (about one million people); a century later barely 20 per cent (almost half a million) spoke it.

The Tudor determination to have an united realm meant that at the Reformation the Welsh Church became part of the Church of England. Since the large majority of the people had no English, in order to ensure the success of the Reformation *The Book of Common Prayer* and the New Testament were translated into Welsh in 1567 and the whole Bible in 1588. Paradoxically, these publications helped to standardize and safeguard the Welsh language, and ensure its continuous use in public life.

From the eighteenth century onwards until the latter part of the following century no Welsh-speaking bishops were appointed. Many of them were absent from their dioceses for much of the time and the Church lacked leadership. It was hampered also by an ill-educated and badly paid clergy, who were often forced to take a number of parishes in order to earn a living. The Methodist Revival of the 1730s onwards, which was separate from the Wesleyan movement, transformed the religious life of Wales, leading to a new enthusiasm and fervour. Although all the original leaders were members of the Established Church it was impossible to contain the movement within Anglicanism. The Calvinistic Methodist Church came into being in 1811 and the older Congregational and Baptist churches had also grown considerably.

By 1850, with the growth of population already noted, four out of every five practising Christians in Wales were members of one of the Nonconformist churches, i.e. outside the Established Church. There was a growing resentment of the status and privilege of that Church and so began a movement to disestablish the Church. Eventually a Parliamentary bill was passed in 1914, although it was not implemented until 1920. In the meantime, from the 1860s onwards a number of outstanding, reforming bishops had been appointed who did much to revive the life of the Anglican Church. New parishes were established, with many churches being built in the urban areas; much better educated and enthusiastic parish clergy were nurtured so that in the decades before Disestablishment the Anglican Church became considerably stronger.

The Church in Wales

In 1920 the Welsh dioceses became independent of Canterbury. Two new dioceses were formed in south Wales and the six dioceses formed a new, separate province under the title 'The Church in Wales'. Henceforth the six bishops, and the Archbishop who would be one of the six, were to be elected by a college made up of clergy and laity drawn from the whole province. The Church was to be synodically governed by a body in which laity were to outnumber clergy by two to one. A constitution was drawn up for the Church, which would only be changed if a two-thirds majority was obtained in all three houses of the Governing Body, comprising the bishops, clergy and lay members. The synodical system was embraced at diocesan and parochial level. The finances and property of the Church were vested in a central Representative Body. In the course of time the Church in Wales has drawn up its own prayer book. It is fully committed to the bilingual principle. In the Welsh-speaking areas of north and west Wales most parishes have services in the Welsh language.

In its Catechism the Church in Wales defines itself as 'the ancient Church of this land, catholic and reformed'. The element of continuity is strongly felt, as it still uses the ancient parish churches and cathedrals; the catholic emphasis is expressed through its retention of the traditional threefold ministry of bishop, priest and deacon, of the creeds as a summary of belief and of liturgical worship and the traditional sacramental system; the reformed emphasis is seen in the centrality of Scripture, the use of the vernacular languages in worship and the use of the Bible as the chief authority for doctrine. The Church in Wales is the strongest of the Welsh churches, with over 100,000 members, 610 parishes and 660 stipendiary clergy.

The Church in Wales is fully involved in the movement for Christian unity, being a member with ten other Churches, including the Roman Catholic Church, of Churches Together in Wales. In 1975 it entered into a covenant relationship with the Methodist Church, the United Reformed Church, the Presbyterian Church of Wales and a group of Baptist churches to pray and work together for an united church. It is also a signatory to the Porvoo Agreement with the Lutheran Churches of the Nordic and Baltic lands, and is a member of the Council of Churches of Britain and Ireland, the Conference of European Churches and the World Council of Churches.

The *Conseil Permanent Luthéro-Reformé*

Werner Jurgensen

Origins and Structures

The French Lutheran and Reformed churches have long been aware of a common calling in the context of the social and religious life of their country. For a long time they have had to coexist with a Roman Catholic Church that was numerically and politically dominant. In this difficult situation, they have felt themselves called to mutual solidarity, and at the same time to witness anew to their common faith.

This common calling presented, and indeed still presents, a twofold challenge:

- We have essentially before us two different traditions, stemming from the Reformation of the sixteenth century, Calvinism (which has assumed the name 'Reformed') and Lutheranism (often referring back to the Augsburg Confession).

- The political history of our country has meant that the networks of relationships, the law, and the cultural identity of Alsace and Lorraine (or more precisely the Département of la Moselle) have developed differently from the other regions of France.

In 1905, when Protestantism was very fragmented and dispersed, a need for rapprochement was felt, and this led to the creation of the Protestant Federation of France. But as the Federation became open to the diversity of other streams of Protestantism, it became apparent that a closer proximity between the Lutheran and Reformed churches permitted and called for closer co-operation. Between 1960 and 1968, common theological work led to the 'Theses on Ordination' (1961). It culminated in the adoption of the 'Theses of Lyon', which express the agreement of these churches on the word of God, baptism and Holy Communion. In due course, these were to be consolidated in a broader European context in the Leuenberg Agreement (1973).

In 1969, there was a proposal that these churches become one. The 'Draft for Union between the Protestant Churches of France' was the subject of a wide consultation among the churches at every level. This consultation, however, did not give rise to such a union, and people talked for a long time of the 'failure of the Draft'. But in fact, it was not a failure. Though they did not see the point of specific visions of unity, the Lutheran and Reformed Churches were to show themselves determined to keep in close contact and to develop further the common co-operation that was a sign of their effective communion. First of all, the executive councils of the four churches that were involved – the Church of the Augsburg Confession of Alsace and Lorraine (ECAAL), the Evangelical–Lutheran Church of France (EELF), the Reformed Church of Alsace and Lorraine (ERAL) and the Reformed Church of France (ERF) – took it upon themselves to ensure that there was contact between them (people spoke of the meeting of the 'Four Offices'). In 1972, a Lutheran–Reformed Standing Council (*Conseil Permanent Luthéro-Reformé* – CPLR) was given permanent oversight of this mission of consolidation and co-operation, and the task was given new concreteness both at the heart of the Protestant Federation of France and alongside it. The fundamental aim of the CPLR is to make manifest the communion that exists between the member churches.

Today, the possibility of enlarging this communion to include a fifth church, the Union of the Reformed Evangelical Independent Churches, is being studied, and collaboration with this church is under way. The Council normally meets three times a year; each church is represented by four delegates, who for the most part come from the central committees of the churches. Every four years, a Common Assembly is held, with a larger number of delegates, to provide a focus for common life and to debate a subject of importance.

A further step forward has recently been taken in the creation, in June 1996, of an Infrastructure, which ensures that the CPLR has the legal status that had been lacking to date, and that it is able to manage directly the personnel, finance and areas of work that are entrusted to it by the member churches.

Day-to-day work is directed by an office consisting of four to seven members (currently seven) who do the preparatory work for the meetings of the Council and carry out its decisions. This is a very light structure and at present relies entirely on volunteers, including, notably, its President, but the work is tending to increase with the multiplication of areas of co-operation between the member churches.

The Main Axes of Co-operation

The two essential and visible axes of the inter-church co-operation whose structure is outlined above are ecumenical relations – in particular with the Roman Catholic Church in France – and the ongoing training of ministers.

The concern for ecumenism has been given substance notably in the constitution of the *Comité Mixte catholique-protestant* (Joint Catholic-Protestant Committee). This facilitates pastoral discussion and theological work between the churches of the CPLR and the Roman Catholic Church in France. The ecumenical vocation of the CPLR was confirmed in particular by the establishment, in January 1993, of the Commission for Anglican–Lutheran–Reformed dialogue, whose main remit was to work towards the Reuilly Common Statement in the name of the four churches.

A further manifestation of the ecumenical vocation of the CPLR may be found in the various different ways in which it participates as one body in the life and work of ecumenical organizations such as the World Council of Churches (with particular emphasis on the work of the Faith and Order Commission), the Conference of European Churches, and, of course, the Leuenberg Church Fellowship. The focus of attention of the CPLR is always on co-operation or dialogue between the churches as such, on the pursuit of communion between them and on the deepening of their common mission.

Work on the ongoing training of ministers is ensured by the half-time ministry of a co-ordinator (at present Mlle Anne-Laure Danet, who is a pastor of the Reformed Church of France). Her work is supplemented by pastoral training through the French branch of 'Clinical Pastoral Training' and by some common sessions during the initial training of ministers. This training in common is an important factor in strengthening contacts between ministers of the four churches and in the renewal of their ministry.

From 1988, catechesis has been added to the responsibilities of the CPLR with the creation of a catechetical platform common to the four churches. In 1990, this became part of the *Société des Ecoles du Dimanche* (the Society of Sunday Schools), which was restructured specifically to serve the churches of the CPLR. This process is almost complete, after discussions which have sometimes been difficult, for this is the point above all where the conception, situations and sensitivities of each church have to be modified in accordance with the common aim of communion and practical collaboration. We have already reached agreement on the 'common orientations for catechesis'.

Other Areas of Co-operation

The Common Assembly which met in October 1993 at Dole with the theme 'Growing in Communion' asked that seven areas should be pursued or opened up. Over and above those already mentioned, it was proposed that there should be:

- a multiplication of signs of communion at local and regional level;

- a closer co-operation in the field of liturgy;

- a reflection and debate on ecclesiology, our structures and the exercise of authority in our churches;

- a theological contribution to the search for closer communion in the Federation of Protestant Churches in France;

- a better system of communications at all levels in our churches.

The last Common Assembly, which met at Glay in October 1997, concentrated on matters of training. It also recommended that the emergence of a common memory of the churches of the CPLR should be fostered and that there should be a common study of the particular traditions of each member church.

The Particularity of the Lutheran–Reformed Communion

Our churches illustrate two models of church unity. The French Protestant Federation is an association of churches, institutions, organizations and movements whose federal bond is very wide and whose diversity is growing. The Lutheran–Reformed Standing Council is a locus of communion between its member churches, which permits and calls for co-operation in such sensitive areas as catechesis and ministerial training, liturgy and theological agreements, the status of ministers and their 'interchangeability' (a minister who is duly recognized by one of the four churches can pursue his or her ministry in any of the three others), full mutual recognition as authentic churches of Jesus Christ and, as a result, full mutual recognition and common celebration of the sacraments of baptism and the Lord's Supper.

Why not 'More'?

Because of this communion, there is no area in which co-operation between churches should *a priori* be impossible. For this reason, we are constantly asked why we do not go further, to structural church union. Two types of answer are given.

With a certain impatience, motivated by the absence of any fundamental spiritual obstacle and by the situation of the churches in the present day, some people maintain that the questions of identity and structure that distinguish our churches from one another are secondary and outmoded. They call for courageous steps towards union.

Others underline the decisive character of the steps that have already been taken; we are in communion, unity is a given. Faced with this fundamental reality, they hold that the continuing existence of distinct identities and structures is not a problem. They call for a manifestation and deepening of the unity which is already given to us, through more extensive forms of collaboration and through obvious signs of mutual recognition.

Both approaches contribute to the progress of unity. They are currently being debated between the two Lutheran and Reformed churches of Alsace and Moselle, where there has been a 'scheme for growing-together' since 1992.

For the moment, the CPLR response is closer to the second approach. Recent and long-standing experience has shown that respect for identity, for sensitivities, and for the capacity for co-operation in our churches contributes to reciprocal trust and sets the surest markers for new progress on the way to unity.

The Lutheran and Reformed Churches of Alsace and Lorraine

Marc Lienhard

In the administrative districts of Upper Rhine, Lower Rhine and Moselle, there are two major Reformation churches: the Church of the Augsburg Conference of Alsace and Lorraine (the Lutheran Church) and the Reformed Church of Alsace and Lorraine. According to church statistics, the Lutheran Church (the ECAAL) had 210,000 members in 1993 and the Reformed Church (the ERAL) 33,000. In Alsace, there are approximately 250,000 Protestants, between one-fifth and one-sixth of the total population. Taken together, the two churches represent around one-third of all French Protestants.

Origins

Through writings and sermons, Luther's message spread very quickly in Alsace. The efforts of Martin Bucer and Wolfgang Capiton in particular won Strasbourg over to the Protestant camp as early as 1524, and other cities followed suit: Mulhouse, Wissembourg, Munster, Colmar and various territories such as the territories of the Lordships of Fleckenstein, Oberbronn, Riquewihr, Diemeringen and Fénétrange, the Palatine lands and numerous villages belonging to knights of the Empire.

From the confessional point of view, 'Bucer's Reformation' stands midway between those of Luther and Zwingli. After 1530, however, Bucer drew closer to Luther (Conford of Wittenberg, 1536). During the second half of the sixteenth century, Lutheran orthodoxy triumphed in Strasbourg under Jean Marbach and Jean Pappus. With the exception of Mulhouse and the Palatine lands, which were of Reformed allegiance, the other newly Protestant territories in general followed the example of Strasbourg. The Augsburg Confession became the doctrinal standard. Spirituality – prayers, hymns, imagery – was coloured by Lutheranism.

On through the Centuries

From the sixteenth century to the beginning of the nineteenth, Protestant Christians in Alsace were to be found in some 40 territorial churches, which were governed by ecclesiastical ordinances that were often restrictive. Political and religious authorities concerned themselves as much with the teaching of catechesis and homiletics as with maintaining strict discipline among the faithful. Strasbourg was particularly influential – that was where the majority of ministers received their theological training and the scene of the activities of famous classical theologians such as Jean and Sebastien Schmidt, and Jean Conrad Dannhauer. From the end of the seventeenth century, the impact of Pietism, promoted by the Alsatian Philippe Jacques Spener, and of the Enlightenment, gradually transformed Protestant sensibility and the waves in which the gospel was transmitted. Jean-Frederic Oberlin embodied this new mode of faith and life.

After the upheaval of the Revolution, the Organic Articles passed by Napoleon I in 1802 reorganized Protestant ecclesiastical institutions. The Lutherans were brought together in a Church of the Augsburg Confession with five, then seven, Inspections. These institutions still exist today. Those of a Reformed persuasion were grouped together into three Consistories: Bischwiller, Strasbourg and Mulhouse, to which were added a little later Metz and Sainte-Marie-aux-Mines. The Reformed Consistories remained independent until 1895, when they regrouped, forming a synod which was given official status in 1905.

In the nineteenth century, differences of emphasis in Alsatian Protestantism threatened to tear it apart. On the one hand, the still dominant liberalism which sought to link faith and culture, and favoured a non-dogmatic Christianity (F. Bruch, G. Baum, E. Reuss); on the other, the Pietist Awakening and the Lutheran confessional revival: F. Haerter stressed the importance of conversion, personal piety and works; F. Horning laid emphasis on doctrine, the Lutheran tradition with its hymns and confession of faith, and ecclesiology.

Confronted with the onset of secularization and the social problems linked with the Industrial Revolution, Protestants created new diaconal institutions (diaconal orders, orphanages, hospitals, and so on), invented new forms of evangelization and training (youth movements, home missions), and intensified their missionary activity.

From the Nineteenth to the Twentieth Centuries

The three Franco-German wars each brought about the departure of a certain number of ministers, thus impoverishing the churches. They also contributed to the administrative separation of the ECAAL and the ERAL from the Evangelical–Lutheran Church of France and the Reformed Church of France. Despite all this, the local institutions survived various crises. The separation of Church and State, which was introduced in France in 1905, was not extended to Alsace when Alsace was reincorporated into France in 1918. Ministers therefore continue to be paid by the State, and religious instruction is given in schools. It was only during the years of annexation by Germany, from 1940 to 1945, that churches were set apart from the official regime. In 1911 and again in 1970, there were projects for structural reform within the Lutheran Church.

The impact of certain theologians such as Karl Barth, Dietrich Bonhoeffer and Paul Tillich, the movements of biblical and liturgical renewal, the recent emergence of the charismatic movement, all these bring enrichment to the traditional Protestant ethos. As a result, ministers and parishes representing styles and options that are often divergent no longer experience the theological confrontations that typified their predecessors. Less interested in purely dogmatic debates, they devote their energies to revival, to the enrichment of worship, and to realizing a more effective community life; they set out to form and to educate the faithful, and to promote the social involvement of Christians and of the church with those who are most disadvantaged.

New forms of being the Church are becoming manifest: Protestant gatherings, retreats and training sessions, and witness by means of the mass media. Recent history is also lived out under the sign of ecumenism; relations with Roman Catholics have improved. In token of this, in 1971, 'eucharistic hospitality' for couples with different confessional allegiances was given official approval by the Roman Catholic Diocese and the Protestant synods. The Jubilee of the Augsburg Confession in 1980 and the anniversary of Luther's birth in 1983 were in many cases celebrated in common with groups of Roman Catholics.

Institutions and Doctrines

The Church of the Augsburg Confession of Alsace and Lorraine (Lutheran)

The Lutheran Church, with 246 pastoral positions, has 203 parishes, some with annexed charges, and three auxiliary parishes. The parishes are grouped into 40 Consistories and seven Inspections: Temple-Neuf, Saint-Thomas, Saint-Guillaume, Bouxviller, La Petite-Pierre, Wissembourg and Colmar. The Higher Consistory and the Directorate are the governing bodies of the Lutheran Church. The Higher Consistory, an assembly with 25 members, is the locus of doctrinal and legislative authority in the church. The executive organ, the Directorate, has five members: its functions are administrative and disciplinary. Its task is to put into practice developments initiated by the Higher Consistory. The President of the Directorate is assisted in his functions by two general secretaries.

Church life is not limited to parish life; it also finds expression in retreat centres, youth movements, chaplaincies, diaconal work, mission at home and abroad, the presence of the church in the mass media, etc.

The Lutheran Church is rooted in the Reformation of the sixteenth century. It affirms that Holy Scripture is its sole authority in matters of faith; and that justification by faith is the most important element of this. In order to maintain the centrality of Holy Scripture and to gather the whole church around one Confession of Faith, the traditional texts have had an important place in the teaching of the church. And so the Lutheran Church places particular emphasis on the creeds of the Early Church, on the Augsburg Confession and Luther's Small Catechism. Whether these references are explicit or implicit, they do not exclude the richness that comes from a diversity of theological emphases, especially from pastoral experience.

Various theological texts which have been adopted by the Higher Consistory interpret these common references for today's world.

The Reformed Church of Alsace and Lorraine

The Reformed Church has 52 parishes and 60 pastoral charges. The Consistories (Strasbourg, Sainte-Marie-aux-Mines, Mulhouse, Bischwiller, Metz) and their institutions are of greater importance than the Consistories in the Lutheran Church. The Synod and the Synodical

Council are the governing bodies of the Reformed Church. In 1970, the position of President of the Synodical Council was officially created.

The Reformed Church also stems from the Reformation of the sixteenth century. Many parishes date back to the time when areas were repopulated by Protestants after the Thirty Years War, or from the industrial expansion of the nineteenth century. This church sees itself as following the 'Reformed' tradition of Calvin. (John Calvin lived in Strasbourg from 1538 to 1541 and participated in the organization of the Reformed community, of which he was the first pastor.) It is referred to in old documents as the Church of the Helvetic Confession, and thus associated with a confession of faith which was drawn up in Switzerland in 1566. When it officially came into being in 1905, the Reformed Church did not adopt any particular confession of faith. But in 1987, the Synod of the Reformed Church recognized in the 'Declaration of Faith of the Reformed Church of France' of 1939 an expression of its faith. This text explicitly refers to the Apostles' creed, the ecumenical creeds and the confession of faith of the Reformation, notably the Confession of La Rochelle.

Relations between the Lutheran and Reformed Churches of Alsace and Lorraine

The two churches, despite their differences in tradition, have in many respects succeeded in achieving an increasingly close collaboration with one another, which is both useful and necessary. The differences between Lutheran and Reformed which were traditionally focused on the interpretation of Holy Communion have been resolved in a new consensus. Agreements such as the Theses of Lyon and the Theses of Liebfrauenberg and the Leuenberg Agreement illustrate very well the common faith of the two traditions and have made possible, for several decades now, numerous contacts at different levels of the Church's life. From 1969 on the officers of the ECAAL and the ERAL have met in a Common Council. Over the years, these meetings have become more regular and frequent, to the extent that the Common Council now deals with practically all the commissions, services and ministries that are above and beyond parish level in the two churches, and the Higher Consistory of the ECAAL and the Synod of the ERAL meet once a year as a Common Assembly.

Despite some different sensitivities between the two traditions, focused especially on church organization, the ECAAL and the ERAL, whose central offices have operated under the same roof since 1989, assume a common responsibility today for all Protestant witness in the region, and for the various contributory activities (over and above the witness of individual churches): chaplaincies in schools, hospitals and prisons, home and foreign mission, catechesis, youth work, training and media work.

The Evangelical–Lutheran Church of France

A Short History

From 1541, the ideas of the Reformation came from neighbouring Switzerland to penetrate the territory of Montbéliard, which was also a neighbour of Alsace. But at that time this region belonged to the Duke of Württemberg, who imposed Lutheranism upon it; this was the only French-speaking region in the world to adhere, from the sixteenth century onwards, to the Lutheran Reformation. The territory of Montbéliard, which was annexed by France in 1793, had a majority Protestant population until the nineteenth century. Then a considerable industrial expansion brought an influx of Roman Catholics and Muslims, so that today Lutherans constitute no more than a tenth of the population; they remain, however, very active in the economic, political and cultural life of the region.

In Paris, Lutheranism took root with the embassy chapels – first the Swedish (1626), then the Danish. From 1742, services were also conducted in French, but not until 1808 was a Lutheran church officially established, attached to Strasbourg. Today, while the Paris conurbation has more than 10 million inhabitants, one per cent are Protestants and one per thousand Lutheran.

The loss of Alsace after the 1870 war forced French Lutheranism to reorganize itself. The two regional churches of Montbéliard and Paris came together to form the Evangelical–Lutheran Church of France (EELF), which has been separated by law from the State, like the other French churches, since 1905.

The Situation Today

Eighty churches, grouped into 24 parishes; 30 ministers, of whom several have regional responsibilities (chaplaincies, leading Bible study); a retreat centre (Glay) and involvement with hospitals and the care of old people; around 30,000 members; such is the current situation of the regional church – also known as the Inspection – of Montbéliard.

The regional Church of Paris – which in theory covers nine-tenths of France – consists in fact of around ten parishes in Paris, around ten in the suburbs, one in Lyon, one in Nice, and quite recently, one in Marseille: in total, 10,000 members and around twenty ministers. It lays a particular emphasis on liturgy and, with its Home Mission, on evangelization.

Structures

The spiritual and material life of each parish is the responsibility of a Presbyteral Council, with lay members elected for six years and one or more parish ministers. Several parishes form a Consistory (five in Montbéliard, three in Paris), which facilitates close collaboration.

Each of the two regional churches has a synod, which meets at least once a year, in which all the parishes are represented, as well as special ministerial appointments. The Synod is concerned with the life of the church at regional level, and transmits its recommendations to the General Synod. It elects a Synodical Council, presided over by a lay person, which deals with current affairs. In the case of the Synod and Council, two-thirds of the representatives are lay and one-third pastors; as far as is practicable, this is also the case with the specialized commissions (Ministry, Mission, Catechesis, Youth Work, etc).

For each region there is also an Ecclesiastical Inspector, who is elected for five years by the Synod, with the possibility of being re-elected immediately for one further term of office. The Ecclesiastical Inspector exercises a ministry of unity, of oversight, of advice and of pastoral visitation; he is pastor to pastors and other ministers, and presides at ordinations.

The General Synod of the EELF, the collegial layer of church government, normally meets once a year. Two-thirds of its representatives are lay people and one-third are pastors. It is responsible for drawing up the constitution, laws and liturgical texts and for ensuring that these are respected, and also for giving the basic orientation for church life, witness and teaching. It elects an Executive Council of sixteen members, which represents it in the intervals between sessions and which manages church affairs.

Relationships

The EELF, together with the other French Lutheran church, the Church of the Augsburg Confession of Alsace and Lorraine, constitutes the National Alliance of Lutheran Churches in France. This holds a common Assembly every two years, which serves as the French national committee of the Lutheran World Federation.

At the national level, the EELF is also a member of the Standing Council of the Lutheran and Reformed Churches (CPLR), the French Protestant Federation, and the Council of Christian Churches in France.

At the international level, the EELF is a founder member of the Conference of European Churches, the Lutheran World Federation and the World Council of Churches.

The Reformed Church of France: An Historical Introduction

Marianne Carbonnier-Burkard

The Reformed Church of France came into being officially in 1938, when the two church unions which brought together the great majority of the Reformed churches regrouped themselves around a common Declaration of Faith and *Discipline* (Book of Order). In reality it has inherited four centuries of history.

The Sixteenth Century

The beginnings were Protestant communities which came into being here and there from 1540 onwards, little groups of people who read the gospel in French, separating themselves from the traditional Church, which they judged to be faithless, in the wake of the ideas of Luther and the Swiss theologians. Relentlessly pursued as isolated heretics, these communities were fragile. Under the influence of John Calvin, the reformer of Geneva, there was a mutation in the 1550s. Ministers sent from Geneva spread Calvinist Reformed doctrine and an ecclesial model structured around 'ministries' – preachers (pastors), 'elders' (lay people with disciplinary functions according to Matthew 18.15-18) and deacons. Then the first churches constituted according to Calvin's proposals came into being. In 1559, they adopted a common confession of faith – the Confession of Faith of La Rochelle, as it was to be called – and a common *Discipline*, which set out the internal ordering of the churches, all equal, and their regular assemblies, the 'synods' attended by ministers and elders.

This doctrinal and ecclesial framework led to an extraordinary flowering of Reformed churches over a few years, until, towards 1560, the number of members could be estimated at two million (out of a total population of 18 million). But only after eight wars of religion, in 1598, were the Reformed given more than passing legal recognition. By the Edict of Nantes they were guaranteed liberty of conscience and a qualified freedom of worship.

The Seventeenth Century

For almost a century the Reformed – no more than 1.2 million people – lived under the regime of the Edict of Nantes, which integrated them into French society. However, from the reign of Louis XIV onwards, and especially from 1680, there were multiple restrictions on their freedom, culminating in 1685, following a massive campaign of forced conversions, in the Revocation of the Edict of Nantes. Protestant churches were razed to the ground, meetings proscribed, ministers banned, emigration forbidden, and it was obligatory to have children catechized in the Roman Catholic Church. The aim was to suppress the 'allegedly Reformed religion' in the French kingdom, in order to reunite all the king's subjects in one and the same religion.

The Eighteenth Century

The next hundred years was the time of the 'wilderness' (*Désert*) – of the wanderings of the faithful who were deprived of ministers and places of worship and of the right to be Protestant.

Up to about 1760, a time of repression by the law, this 'wilderness' could be styled 'heroic'; in peril of their lives, 'preachers' and prophets preached the forbidden word in secret. Some called for violent resistance in the name of 'freedom of conscience', as was the case during the war of the Camisards (1702–4).

Disapproving of disorder and violence, Antoine Court undertook the 'restoration' of the wilderness churches from 1715: he saw to it that recognized ministers had theological training and that a code of discipline and synods were re-established.

This organization was clandestine but, from 1760 on, the Reformed churches settled into a situation of *de facto* toleration, with occasional local spurts of strict application of the law. Not until 1787 did the Edict of 'Toleration' afford civil status to the Reformed; that is, the right to exist as 'non-Catholics' in the realm. It was not until the French Revolution that the freedom of conscience of all citizens was recognized (1789), followed by freedom of worship (1791), which was stifled during the Terror (1793–5).

The Nineteenth Century

Though greatly weakened, the Reformed communities continued to exist, with approximately 750,000 members in a French population of 28 million. In 1802, Bonaparte included them among the religious denominations (*cultes*) that were 'recognized' by the State, and they continued to live under the Concordat until 1905.

The nineteenth century left lasting marks on French Reformed Protestantism. From 1852 onwards, there was organization into 'parishes', with 'elders' elected by universal male suffrage, and, at the level above, into 'districts'. New theologies developed, that of the 'Awakening' and that of 'liberalism', on the basis of which the opposing views of 'evangelicals' (or 'orthodox') and 'liberals' formed themselves – particularly at the Assembly of 1872. 'Asylums', hospices and Protestant schools were created.

With their complete integration into French society in the Third Republic, many Protestants were to be found in the political and administrative personnel of the new Republican government, challenged by the Roman Catholic Church.

The Twentieth Century

The Law of Separation of Church and State, passed in 1905, made all churches legally private associations without any material assistance from the State. The Reformed churches split into three church 'unions', owing to the theological cleavages between 'evangelicals', 'liberals' and 'evangelical Christian socialists'.

Hence, quite quickly, came projects for unification of these church unions. These led, in 1938, to the formation of the Reformed Church of France (which nonetheless did not include a minority of the Evangelical Reformed churches which, in 1948, assumed the name of Independent Evangelical Reformed Churches). The French Reformed Church has as its foundation document a Declaration of Faith to which every minister must subscribe. A prefatory rubric clarifies the intention of this affirmation: 'Without committing yourself to its formulations to the letter, you will proclaim the message of salvation which they express; and so the faithful preaching of the gospel will be maintained.'

93

Perceptions of the Reformed Church of France

Michel Bertrand

A Minority Church that is Dispersed in a Secularized Society

Despite fluctuations over the centuries, Protestantism has always been a minority tradition in France. This reality, along with a history of persecution, has had a profound impact on the Reformed Church of France and is still determinative of its life, its theology and the programmes it undertakes. During the twentieth century, it has experienced a drop in numbers, along with the other historic churches, and this has accentuated its numerical weakness.

Its minority status is made worse by the fact that it is so scattered. This reality, which is not merely a matter of geography, is often experienced as a negative factor, raising questions about the identity and visibility of our church. But it also gives rise to new styles of community living which make it possible to witness, despite the difficulties.

This sense of being dispersed is all the more acute for the fact that society itself has become pluralist and has lost the common values which safeguard community life. There is a search for meaning in a secularized world, a need for landmarks in a situation of uncertainty.

A Church with Roots which Changes and Is Renewed

Suddenly, today, new ways of belonging to the Church are emerging, embodying new expectations. In the situation of a minority diaspora, these may provide an opportunity for strengthening and renewing contacts with Protestants who are distanced from the Church, and with people who are not the product of the historic Reformed group. These are not members in the traditional sense of the word, but they choose specific occasions or significant moments in their lives to listen to the gospel and experience something of the church community. Through its attentiveness, its welcome, its pastoral care and preaching, the church strives to help them place their lives before God. Signs of growth and renewal are then given. And if our church corresponds less and less to the little Reformed community of history, it is stimulated and encouraged by all the newcomers, more numerous than we imagine, who take part in its life and witness.

A Missionary Church which Witnesses in Society

But if evangelization begins at the threshold of our communities, it also summons us to speak and act in the public arena. In local churches there is a new sense of missionary aspiration, a desire to inscribe the news of salvation at the heart of history, an effort to depart from the fears and inhibitions, the inwardness and discouragement, which can stem from our situation as a dispersed minority. The styles of such intervention in the public arena are certainly diverse. They cover all forms of proclamation of the word and of service, notably in the broken places of our society.

In the content of the secular State, which it supports, our church has made its voice heard in the great debates of society. It is not a question of indiscriminate intervention, nor of being constituted a pressure group, but of being present, as participants, in a way that is neither magisterial nor marginal. This requires of us both conviction and tolerance, in order to share the certainties we have received in Christ without believing that we have all the answers.

A Church which Renews and Broadens its Common Life

This implies that we are living out our presbyterian-synodical government in a dynamic new way: strengthening local church life and at the same time enhancing the profile of the synodical level, where communion is expressed and solidarity experienced in concrete terms.

We ought by all possible means to show a creative desire to communicate and collaborate with one another, by paying one another visits, by meeting together, by sharing mutual experiences, by strengthening indirect relationships, and by setting up working networks on common projects and objectives.

In so doing, Protestantism can offer our broken society, lacking in cohesion and solidarity, a model of unity in diversity, a *modus vivendi* which does not suppress differences but which is enriched by them.

This implies also that we should not claim unilaterally to be the Church. Part of our identity is to be with others, with other sections of Protestantism, in ecumenical dialogue and international relations, in all the networks and organisms that serve the universal Church.

A Church in Debate which Deepens its Convictions

Our witness will only be solid and relevant if we foster debate and accept constructive confrontation. The diversity which exists in our churches is not an excuse for laziness, nor a juxtaposition of diverse opinions that are equally acceptable, but a demanding reality that summons us to exchange and debate.

With freedom and respect, we should mutually challenge one another on our assertions, and, without being at daggers drawn, accept that matters be reopened which we thought had been settled once and for all. Without this our convictions on both sides are at risk of becoming superficial.

It is when the vitality of theological debate weakens in the Church that its unity is threatened and its witness becomes insignificant, lacking in pertinence and consistency. We need places where we can exchange views and debate freely, places where awareness can be deepened, where differing convictions can confront one another and shared convictions be constructed, within the context of our common task of deepening our knowledge of Scripture.

Doctrinal Statements
and Declarations of Assent

1. Church of England

CANON C15: OF THE DECLARATION OF ASSENT

1 (1) The Declaration of Assent to be made under this Canon shall be in the form set out below:

Preface

The Church of England is part of the One, Holy, Catholic and Apostolic Church worshipping the one true God, Father, Son and Holy Spirit. It professes the faith uniquely revealed in the Holy Scriptures and set forth in the catholic creeds, which faith the Church is called upon to proclaim afresh in each generation. Led by the Holy Spirit, it has borne witness to Christian truth in its historic formularies, the Thirty-nine Articles of Religion, the Book of Common Prayer and the Ordering of Bishops, Priests and Deacons. In the declaration you are about to make will you affirm your loyalty to this inheritance of faith as your inspiration and guidance under God in bringing the grace and truth of Christ to this generation and making Him known to those in your care?

Declaration of Assent

I, A B, do so affirm, and accordingly declare my belief in the faith which is revealed in the Holy Scriptures and set forth in the catholic creeds and to which the historic formularies of the Church of England bear witness; and in public prayer and administration of the sacraments, I will use only the forms of service which are authorized or allowed by Canon.

2.   Church of Ireland

a.   THE CONSTITUTION OF THE CHURCH OF IRELAND, ADOPTED BY THE GENERAL CONVENTION IN THE YEAR 1870: PREAMBLE AND DECLARATION

In the name of the Father and of the Son, and of the Holy Ghost. Amen: Whereas it hath been determined by the Legislature that on and after the lst day of January, 1871, the Church of Ireland shall cease to be established by law; and that the ecclesiastical law of Ireland shall cease to exist as law save as provided in the 'Irish Church Act, 1869', and it hath thus become necessary that the Church of Ireland should provide for its own regulation:

We, the archbishops and bishops of this the Ancient Catholic and Apostolic Church of Ireland, together with the representatives of the clergy and laity of the same, in General Convention assembled in Dublin in the year of our Lord God one thousand eight hundred and seventy, before entering on this work, do solemnly declare as follows:-

I

1.   The Church of Ireland doth, as heretofore, accept and unfeignedly believe all the Canonical Scriptures of the Old and New Testament, as given by inspiration of God, and containing all things necessary to salvation; and doth continue to profess the faith of Christ as professed by the Primitive Church.

2.   The Church of Ireland will continue to minister the doctrine, and sacraments, and the discipline of Christ, as the Lord hath commanded; and will maintain inviolate the three orders of bishops, priests or presbyters, and deacons in the sacred ministry.

3.   The Church of Ireland, as a reformed and Protestant Church, doth hereby reaffirm its constant witness against all those innovations in doctrine and worship, whereby the primitive Faith hath been from time to time defaced or overlaid, and which at the Reformation this Church did disown and reject.

II

The Church of Ireland doth receive and approve *The Book of the Articles of Religion*, commonly called the Thirty-nine Articles, received and approved by the archbishops and bishops and the rest of the clergy of Ireland in the synod holden in Dublin, AD 1634; also, *The Book of Common Prayer and Administration of the Sacraments and other Rites and Ceremonies of the Church, according to the use of the Church of Ireland; and the Form and Manner of Making, Ordaining and Consecrating of Bishops, Priests and Deacons*, as approved and adopted by the synod holden in Dublin, AD 1662, and hitherto in use in this Church. And this Church will continue to use the same, subject to such alterations only as may be made therein from time to time by the lawful authority of the Church.

III

The Church of Ireland will maintain communion with the sister Church of England, and with all other Christian Churches agreeing in the principles of this Declaration; and will set forward, so far as in it lieth, quietness, peace, and love, among all Christian people.

IV

The Church of Ireland, deriving its authority from Christ, Who is the Head over all things to the Church, doth declare that a General Synod of the Church of Ireland, consisting of the archbishops and bishops, and of representatives of the clergy and laity, shall have chief legislative power therein, and such administrative power as may be necessary for the Church, and consistent with its episcopal constitution.

b.   DECLARATION FOR SUBSCRIPTION

I, AB, do hereby solemnly declare that –

(1) I approve and agree to the Declaration prefixed to the statutes of the Church of Ireland, passed at the General Convention in the year of our Lord one thousand eight hundred and seventy.

(2) I assent to the Thirty-nine Articles of Religion, and to the Book of Common Prayer, and of the ordering of Bishops, Priests and Deacons. I believe the doctrine of the Church of Ireland, as therein set forth, to be agreeable to the Word of God; and in public prayer and administration of the sacraments I will use the form in the said Book prescribed, and none other, except so far as shall be allowed by the lawful authority of the Church.

(3) [against simony]

(4) [against pluralism]

(5) [canonical obedience]

(6) I promise to submit myself to the authority of the Church of Ireland, and to the laws and tribunals thereof.

3. Scottish Episcopal Church

DECLARATION OF ASSENT

I, . . . do solemnly make the following Declaration. I assent to the Book of Common Prayer and to the Ordering of Bishops, Priests and Deacons. I believe the doctrine of the Church as therein set forth to be agreeable to the Word of God, and in public prayer and administration of the Sacraments I will use the form in the said Book prescribed and none other except so far as shall be allowed by lawful authority in this Church.

4. Church in Wales

DECLARATION AND UNDERTAKING

I, J... S... do solemnly declare my belief in the Faith which is revealed in the Holy Scriptures and set forth in the Catholic Creeds and to which the historic formularies, namely: the Thirty-nine Articles of Religion, the Book of Common Prayer and the Ordering of Bishops, Priests and Deacons, as published in 1662, bear witness; and in public prayer and administration of the sacraments,

I will use only the forms of service which are allowed by lawful authority, and none other.

And I hereby undertake to be bound by the Constitution of the Church of Wales, and to accept, submit to, and carry out any sentence of judgement which may at any time by passed upon me by the Archbishop, Diocesan Bishop or any Court of the Church in Wales.

5. The Church of the Augsburg Conference of Alsace and Lorraine and The Evangelical–Lutheran Church of France

The confessional basis of the two French Lutheran churches is principally set out in the ecumenical creeds, the Augsburg Confession of 1530 and Luther's Small Catechism. The affirmation at ordination contains, in the case of each church, the following formula:

> *The Ecclesiastical Inspector addresses the ordinand:* God has called you to serve him as a pastor. In response to the call of our Lord Jesus Christ, in the communion of the Universal Church, are you ready to carry out faithfully the ministry that has been entrusted to you, proclaiming the good news of Jesus Christ as contained in holy Scripture, celebrating the sacraments instituted by our Lord, in conformity with the confessions of faith that are recognized by our church?

> *The ordinand replies:* I am. Jesus Christ is Lord, may he be my helper.

6. The Reformed Church of France

The Statutes of the National Union of Worship Associations of the Reformed Church of France reconcile the traditional structures of the Church with the Law of Separation of Church and State. Every local church, each local, regional and national council, every minister in the Reformed Church of France, is called upon to affirm the faith of the Church as it is set out in the Preamble to the Statutes.

> . . . In its firm desire to be a faithful instrument of God the Redeemer in all its activities, the Reformed Church of France sets the following Declaration of Faith at the heart of its life and organization.

In confessing its faith in the sovereignty of God and in Christ as Saviour, the Reformed Church of France is moved, first of all, to give thanks and praise to God, the Father of all mercies.

Faithful to the principles of faith and freedom on which it is founded, in the fellowship of the universal Church, it affirms the witness borne to the one Christian faith by successive formulations and declarations of faith, in the Apostles' creed, the ecumenical creeds and the confessions of faith of the Reformation, notably the Confession of Faith of La Rochelle; its faith springs from the central revelation of the gospel: For God so loved the world that he gave his only Son, so that everyone who believes in him may not perish but may have eternal life.

With its Fathers and its Martyrs, and with all the churches which arose in the Reformation, it affirms the supreme authority of Holy Scripture, discerned under the guidance of the Holy Spirit, for the faith and conduct of all God's people;

it proclaims the salvation of a fallen humanity by grace, through faith in Jesus Christ, the only Son of God, who was delivered up for our sins, and raised from the dead for our justification;

it grounds its teaching and its worship on the great Christian events proclaimed in the gospel, represented in the sacraments, celebrated in its services and expressed in its liturgy.

In obedience to its divine calling, it proclaims to a sinful world the gospel of repentance and forgiveness, of new birth, of holiness and eternal life.

Under the guidance of the Holy Spirit, it demonstrates its faith through works; it labours in prayer for the awakening of souls, to make the unity of the Body of Christ manifest, and for peace. Through its evangelical and missionary work, through its struggles against the ills of our society, it prepares the way of the Lord, looking ever to that day when, through the triumph of its Head, the Kingdom of God and his justice will become a present reality.

Unto Him who is able to do exceedingly abundantly above all that we ask or think, according to the power that works in us, unto Him be glory in the Church by Christ Jesus throughout all ages, world without end. Amen.

In the liturgy of recognition of a minister, the officiating minister addresses the candidate as follows:

> Today, . . . , in the communion of the Universal Church, we receive you as servant of Christ in the Reformed Church of France. We will shortly hear its Declaration of Faith. It will remind you of the abiding principles of the Reformation and the facts and truths on which the Church of God is founded. You will subscribe to it joyfully in a free and personal affirmation of your faith. Without committing yourself to the letter of its formulations, you will proclaim the message of salvation that they express. And so the faithful proclamation of Jesus Christ will be maintained according to the apostolic witness and in conformity with the traditions of faith and the Christian life that we have received from our fathers.

7. The Reformed Church of Alsace and Lorraine

a. The confessional basis of the Reformed Church of Alsace and Lorraine is principally located in:

> the ecumenical creeds
> the Confession of Faith of La Rochelle (1559)
> the Heidelberg Catechism (1563)
> the Later Helvetic Confession (1566)

b. In 1987, the ERAL adopted the Declaration of Faith of the Reformed Church of France (1938). It suffices to adapt this text, substituting '*the Reformed Church of Alsace and Lorraine*' for '*the Reformed Church of France*'.

c. The Assent to this Declaration of Faith in the liturgy for the recognition of ministries is formulated in the same way as in the Reformed Church of France.

THE EUCHARIST IN OUR CHURCHES

The Lord's Supper[1]

(Liebfrauenberg, 22 March 1981)

Gathered for the Assembly of the Standing Council of the Lutheran and Reformed Churches of France, we have, once again, gratefully held together a Communion service. Grounded in the witness of the Scriptures, we would like to proclaim today the convictions we share and which are, for us, decisive.

In fellowship with the other European churches which stem from the Reformation, the Reformed and Lutheran churches of France have checked and expressed their fundamental agreement about the Lord's Supper through the Leuenberg Agreement (1973). That agreement had already been expressed in one of the so-called 'Theses of Lyons' (1968). Moreover, their understanding of the mystery of the Lord's Supper has been enriched by other studies from the ecumenical movement.

1. The Lord Jesus Christ approaches men in different ways, making use of the human word, just as much as of the water of baptism or of the bread and wine of the Supper, word and sacrament are for us like the two focal points of an ellipse. They need each other. Like the sacraments, the word is the power of God for the salvation of the world. Conversely, the Lord's Supper is not only an act and a celebration, it is also a visible word given us by the same Lord who makes use here of other elements of his creation so as to make himself present amongst us and pass on to us his gospel. The sacrament is for us more than an appendix to preaching, and preaching more than just an introduction to the sacrament.

---

[1] The French title is 'La Cène du Seigneur.' The word *cène*, from the Latin word for the evening meal, is used in French as a technical word for the Lord's last meal with his disciples when the subject of a painting, and for the Protestant Holy Communion. *Cène* is here rendered by 'Supper', though the word is never used for *souper*, which is the French equivalent of 'supper'. *Sainte-Cène*, which is a purely Protestant word, is translated 'Holy Communion'.

2.   In the Lord's Supper, the meal of the New Covenant, the Lord binds himself to the act of eating and drinking. To communicate to us the grace of his presence, he chose the bread which he invites us to eat and the wine which he invites us to drink. In receiving them, we receive the body of Christ given for us. That presence, which no explanation will ever be able to account for in a completely satisfactory way, is grounded in the promise of Christ. It is not the work of human subjectivity and devotion, but the work of the Holy Spirit.

3.   During the earthly ministry of Jesus, a meal, shared bread, often became tokens of communion between the Son of Man and the children of God. When about to face death, the Lord ate the Passover and instituted the Supper as a sign of his presence among us and of his life given for us. And, from the very beginning of the Church, the witnesses of Christ have testified to his resurrection by continuing to celebrate that meal. They did so as an act of public confession which inaugurates the mission of the Church.

4.   Benefiting by the one perfect sacrifice of Jesus Christ, who died on the cross and is risen from the dead, a sacrifice actualized in the Supper, we give thanks to God and to Christ. Forgiven sinners, we raise our heads to walk in faith and hope. With confidence we pray to God through Jesus Christ, the high priest and intercessor present among us. We lay the world before him, its distress and its hopes. In communion with Christ, we offer ourselves for the service of God and the service of men.

5.   To express that presence of Christ, the celebration of the Supper includes, especially, the following liturgical actions:

   a.   Giving thanks (eucharist), that is praising God. That praise sums up all the gratitude of the Church towards the Father and Creator, as it receives the assurance of salvation thanks to the unique sacrifice of the Son.

   b.   Recalling (*anamnesis*), that is remembering the institution of the Supper and actualizing, through the power of the Holy Spirit, the sacrifice of Christ on the cross, signified in that memorial.

   c.   Invoking the Holy Spirit (*epiclesis*) upon the gathered congregation and on the whole celebration, so that the bread and the cup may serve for the communion between Christ and us.

d.   Interceding for the Church, its faithfulness and unity, for the world and for the future. That prayer is at the same time consecration to the service of the brethren and power of reconciliation between men.

e.   Proclaiming our awaiting of the kingdom.

6.   At Holy Communion, bread and wine remain what they are. Yet, 'they receive a new purpose, that of communicating to us the gift of God in Jesus Christ and expressing that he is really our food and drink' (*Thèse de Lyon*).

7.   It is the Lord himself who invites us to his table and permits us to anticipate the meal of the kingdom. Nonetheless, the question of the human presidency is not indifferent. By asking that the Supper be presided over by an ordained minister of the Church or by somebody who is commissioned by the Church, we want to recall that the eucharistic celebration is not just an individual celebration or that of a particular group, but that through it we are in communion with the universal Church. That communion is affirmed through the unfolding of the liturgy.

8.   This insertion into the universal Church gives us permission to invite all those who confess Jesus Christ crucified and risen for us to share the Eucharist with us.

Thus, when celebrating the Supper we live out the remembrance of the distress and suffering of Christ in his passion, the assurance of his real and secret presence in the power of his resurrection, and the groanings of creation awaiting the kingdom.

Recommendations

The Assembly of the Standing Council of the Lutheran and Reformed Churches of France considers that it must make the following recommendations to the churches:

1.   The churches are invited to diversify their eucharistic practices by maintaining a fruitful tension between order and freedom, tradition and innovation: diversification according to the Church's calendar, eucharistic services of the whole congregation, eucharistic services

for particular groups, participation of children, Holy Communion with a meal preceding or following communion brought to the sick by deacons and elders, etc. . . .

2. The churches must seek separately and together new ways of worship. The celebration of the Supper ought to offer to all who take part an opportunity to live through differently the usual elements of the liturgy of the Sunday service.

3. If it is true that Holy Communion is more frequent than in the past, we must nevertheless be careful to give it a less exceptional character, bind it more strongly to the word.

4. To reach that goal, Holy Communion must be the subject of methodical teaching, not only when catechizing, but also in adult education within the Church. That implies that the papers gathered in issue 4 of *Recherches ecclésiales* be widely circulated and seriously studied.

5. As for the way of dealing with the bread and wine left after the celebration, feelings vary. They do not touch our common faith in the real presence of Christ. But they challenge us all about our different ways of proceeding. Some want to avoid anything that might imply that the elements are sacred. Others think that, due to their purpose during the celebration, the elements must be treated with respect, even after the celebration. All should take care to avoid hurting the feelings of their ecumenical partners.

6. The churches must respect those of their members who, whether for reasons of conscience or for theological reasons, think they must abstain from Communion, or are reticent towards what they feel is a too frequent celebration. The churches will avoid giving those people the feeling that they are excluded or relegated to the margins of the congregation.

7. They will be careful that the celebration of Holy Communion leads to an effective missionary commitment in the widest meaning of the word: life in fellowship with the congregation, *diakonia*, action for justice, evangelization, mission.

[translated by J.-P. Monsarrat]

Anglican Eucharistic Practice

Christopher Hill

Anglican practice, whatever different theologies have been developed within different schools of Anglicanism, has invariably required ordination to the priesthood (or episcopate) for canonical presidency at a Eucharist. Anglican practice since the beginning of the seventeenth century has also mandatorily required an explicit consecration of the eucharistic elements and the reverent consumption of the eucharistic elements after the celebration if they are not required for communion. The following canonical and liturgical extracts make this clear.

B12 OF THE MINISTRY OF THE HOLY COMMUNION

1. No person shall consecrate and administer the holy sacrament of the Lord's Supper unless he shall have been ordained priest by episcopal ordination in accordance with the provisions of Canon C1.

C12 OF HOLY ORDERS IN THE CHURCH OF ENGLAND

1. The Church of England holds and teaches that from the apostles' time there have been these orders in Christ's Church: bishops, priests, and deacons; and no man shall be accounted or taken to be a lawful bishop, priest, or deacon in the Church of England, or suffered to execute any of the said offices, except he be called, tried, examined, and admitted thereunto according to the Ordinal or any form of service alternative thereto approved by the General Synod under Canon B2, authorized by the Archbishops of Canterbury and York under Canon C4A or has had formerly episcopal consecration or ordination in some Church whose orders are recognized and accepted by the Church of England.

THE ORDER FOR HOLY COMMUNION, 1662

Rubric

And if any of the Bread and Wine remain unconsecrated, the Curate shall have it to his own use; but if any remain of that which was consecrated, it shall not be carried out of the Church, but the Priest, and such other of the Communicants as he shall then call unto him, shall, immediately after the Blessing, reverently eat and drink the same.

THE ORDER FOR HOLY COMMUNION, 1980

Note

2. **The President** The president (who, in accordance with the provisions of Canon B12 'Of the Ministry of the Holy Communion', must have been episcopally ordained priest) presides over the whole service. He says the opening Greeting, the Collect, the Absolution, the Peace, and the Blessing; he himself must take the bread, and the cup before replacing them on the holy table, say the Eucharistic Prayer, break the consecrated bread, and receive the sacrament on every occasion. The remaining parts of the service he may delegate to others. When necessity dictates, a deacon or lay person may preside over the Ministry of the Word.

When the Bishop is present, it is appropriate that he should act as president. He may also delegate sections 32–49 to a priest.

Rubric

67 If either or both of the consecrated elements be likely to prove insufficient, the priest himself returns to the holy table and adds more, and consecrates according to the form in section 65, beginning, 'Our Saviour Christ in the same night . . .,' for the bread, and at 'In the same way, after supper our Saviour . . .,' for the cup.

68 Any consecrated bread and wine which is not required for purposes of communion is consumed at the end of the distribution or after the service.

Eucharistic Presidency

All our churches at present are re-examining and discussing questions relating to the selection, training, role and deployment of ministers, both lay and ordained. This is partly because of renewed theological insights into what is meant by the ministry of all the baptized, and partly for practical reasons, such as shortage of resources and pastoral necessity. While the norm in all our churches is that the preaching of the word, the administration of the sacraments, the presidency at worship and the provision of pastoral care are primarily the responsibility of the ordained ministers, they are not all perceived as being in all circumstances confined to the ordained. New patterns of ministry are being developed and tested.

In the Anglican churches in Britain and Ireland there has been a considerable effort to develop lay ministry (the word 'lay' being used commonly to refer to the non-ordained). Two such ministries are those of lay pastoral assistants, who help with pastoral visiting and care, and worship leaders who are authorized to lead services of the word and prayer, but not to preach. The ministry of preaching is, however, undertaken by (lay) Readers, a ministry which has existed for over a century. Readers are lay men and women who are given careful training before being licensed to take services and preach, but not to preside at the Eucharist. In some of the Anglican churches they may be permitted to baptize and can conduct funerals. The licensing includes an act of commissioning, but does not include invocation of the Spirit and laying on of hands and could not, therefore, be described as ordination.

One response to situations of pastoral need is the practice of extended Communion. In this, a deacon or authorized lay eucharistic minister conducts a service for the congregation and provides them with communion from eucharistic elements which have been previously consecrated by a priest at a public celebration of the Eucharist.

A different but significant development has been a great increase in ordaining people to a voluntary (i.e. non-stipendiary) ministry who remain for the most part in their secular work. These non-stipendiary ministers (or NSMs) are ordained to the full ministry of word and sacraments and are usually given pastoral responsibilities. A more recent development in some dioceses in England is to ordain to a voluntary ministry people who are trained locally and are licensed to serve only in a particular locality. These are known as local non-stipendiary ministers or ordained local ministers (OLMs). The training for these forms of ministry, like that for Readers, lasts between two and three years.

In the French Lutheran and Reformed churches the president of the Eucharist (*culte de la Parole et des Sacraments*) is normally an ordained minister. But he or she does not have a monopoly on such a presidency. A plurality of practice stems both from the fact that Protestants in France are unevenly spread over an enormous geographical area, and from theological conviction. Both the Reformed and Lutherans believe that all Christians, by virtue of their baptism, have a part in the one ministry of the whole Church. In their view, each has the capacity to preach the word and celebrate the sacraments, though this does not necessarily mean that they will be called to do so. It is for the Church to discern the gifts, to see that the necessary training is given and to entrust a person with the particular ministry of preaching the word and celebrating the sacraments within the framework of its tradition of church order and discipline.

The French Lutheran and Reformed churches have developed a ministry of Preacher similar to that of lay Reader in the Anglican churches. Proper preparation is required before this service can be undertaken, and the exercise of this ministry is accompanied by in-service training. These churches refuse to make a distinction between word and sacrament (of the Lord's Supper) and do not see why the minister who is officially authorized to preach cannot also be called to preside at a celebration of the Lord's Supper. In many areas of France the ministry of the (lay) Preacher can thus be extended to include the celebration of baptism and the Lord's Supper. The local church is fully involved in the process of selection and nomination of such a person, whose ministry is confirmed by the Regional Council of the church concerned. Often a service of installation (with laying on of hands) takes place as a recognition and confirmation of the ministry of those who are called to this task.

However, although the theological conviction is shared, differences in the situations of the French Lutheran and Reformed churches have led them to adopt different practices. Since their communities are less widely spread over France, the presidency of a (lay) Preacher at the Lord's Supper is rarer in the Lutheran Church. If permission is granted by the relevant authority in the church it is limited to specific occasions. In the Reformed

Church the practice is more widespread. It is seen as an expression of the priesthood of all the baptized and as a vital contribution to the witness of the Church in a diaspora situation.

The practices in the French Lutheran and Reformed churches are not acceptable to the Anglican churches of Britain and Ireland. The General Synod of the Church of England, for example, has recently debated the issue of eucharistic presidency. It stated that lay presidency is incompatible with Anglican tradition, and invited the House of Bishops to make a theological statement. The House of Bishops concluded that there were strong theological arguments for maintaining the inherited tradition as found in the canons and *The Book of Common Prayer.*[1]

Because similar pastoral problems have been met with different theological and pastoral solutions there is a continued need to discuss the question of eucharistic presidency on the basis of our agreement on ministry (cf. *The Reuilly Common Statement*, paras 31 (h) and 46 (a)).

---

[1] *Eucharistic Presidency. A Theological Statement by the House of Bishops of the General Synod* (GS 1248, 1997).

MINISTRY IN OUR CHURCHES

Ministry in the Reformed Church of France

Jean-Pierre Monsarrat

To explain the present provisions and current practice of the Reformed Church of France concerning ministry and ordination, it may be useful to recall briefly some aspects of its history since it was constituted in 1938.

Historical Background

In 1938, four churches united to form the Reformed Church of France. The negotiations that led to unification never touched on the question of ministry. It was understood that all agreed on the matter.

But before long, the question of ministry became an important item on synod agendas, and that remained the case for almost 40 years. Why was that?

First of all, we must take contemporary events into account. With the War and a million and a half French soldiers held prisoner in Germany for nearly five years, many lay people began to play an important part in the life of the church and its congregations. The same could be said of the youth and adult movements. In the prison camps themselves, small groups of Protestants, of all denominations, lived out their church life, holding Sunday services, holding Bible studies and other church activities, and when a chaplain was not available, as was frequently the case, lay people assumed responsibility for these activities.

It became obvious that the life of the Church did not depend on ordained ministers alone; church members could, indeed should, when necessary, play a full part in the worship, training, witness and service of the Church.

If this was obvious, it was also because there was taking place at the same time a biblical revival, in which Suzanne de Dietrich, a lay theologian who spent many years of her life at the Ecumenical Institute, Bossey, played a leading part. Through reading the Pauline Epistles and the Acts of the Apostles, there could be universal agreement that the first churches were rich in all sorts of ministries and ministers.

Furthermore, fresh attention was being drawn to the teaching of Calvin that there were four orders of ministry in the Church – elders, deacons, pastors and theologians.

In 1943 the Professor of Practical Theology at the Theological Faculty in Paris made a speech at the National Synod, in which he pleaded for 'a restoration of ministries in the Reformed Church of France'. 'Let each community be fully alive,' he said, 'that is, may they cease to languish as parasites that draw on the faith of the pastor alone.' He asked Synod to revive the ministry of elders and deacons, and to see that pastors concentrate on preaching the word of God. Instead of keeping for themselves everything that had to be decided or done, pastors should make it possible for members of their congregations to participate fully in the life, worship and witness of the Church. Through baptism, each Christian is called to service. Ministers have simply received gifts to enable them to fulfil specific tasks that are essential to the life of the Church.

Although this speech was rapidly forgotten as such, it touched on many of the ideas that were to fuel debates in the Reformed Church of France up to the beginning of the 1980s.

What track did they take? Where did they end up?

In 1959, the structure of our *Discipline* (Book of Order) was altered. The *Discipline* of 1938, like that of the sixteenth century, began with the ministry of pastors. Doubtless the thinking was that if the Church was edified by the word, the ministry of the word had to come first, before the Church itself. In 1959, in order to underline the fact that it is the Church that receives ministries, and that the pastoral ministry is not the be-all and end-all of its existence, it was decided that the chapters that dealt with the local and national church should precede those that dealt with ministries.

1963 saw the publication of the *Service Book of the Reformed Church of France.* In it there were orders of induction for the councils of the church, presbyteral at local, regional and national level. These liturgies stressed the spiritual calling and responsibility of the councils, the collegial ministry with which they were entrusted by the Lord himself.

There remained the difficult question of the plurality of ministries. The pastoral ministry remained the only ordained ministry in the church and all those who felt called to ministry had to become pastors. As a gesture of protest, young ministers stopped asking for ordination, judging that the ceremony as it was at the time reinforced clericalism and the monopoly of pastors on the life of the church.

I shall leave aside the different attempts that were made to deal with the matter of the diversity of ministries and turn directly to the measures that were taken in the early 1980s.

In 1983, 40 years after the synod mentioned above, the National Synod approved a statement on ministry. Here are some extracts:

> The Reformed Church of France participates in the mission which the Lord entrusts to his own people . . . Through baptism, every member of the Church is called to take part in this mission . . .

> Ministers have functions which vary according to the gifts that each has received and the need to carry out such tasks as are required for the life and service of the community; first amongst these is the need to proclaim to the world and the Church the gospel that is the basis of its faith . . .

> The next two synods adopted the new Ordinal and approved certain changes to the *Discipline*.

Current Order and Practice: A Summary

In the local church, the universal priesthood means that the community as a whole, and each member of the church in particular, are called to play their part in the ministry of the whole church. To enable that ministry to be exercised in worship, training, witness, serving the sick and the poor, etc., there is a need for a diversity of activities and responsibilities. It falls to the Presbyteral Council, with the minister or ministers, to exercise leadership of the local church; and so it is called to discern, arouse, recognize and co-ordinate these responsibilities and tasks that are carried out in its name by church members either internally within the church or elsewhere.

As a corporate body governed by the National Synod, the Reformed Church of France recognizes two types of ministries.

1. The ministries exercised collegially by the presbyteral councils, the national and regional synods, and the regional and national councils. The elected members of these councils are not ministers in their own right. They participate in a collegial ministry. If I am not mistaken, this perception is not characteristic of the Presbyterian churches, where an elder is, individually, a minister of the Church. The lay members of our councils are elected for periods of three or six years, after which, if they are not re-elected, they have no particular position or status in the local church.

2. The ministries entrusted to individual men and women, who are authorized by the National Synod; in practice this is done by the Ministries Commission with delegated authority from the National Synod. These people, and they alone, are ministers of the Reformed Church of France. The great majority are pastors to whom is entrusted the ministry of word and sacraments, which is first amongst ministries, but not superior to the others. There are many other possible ways of exercising ministry, however: there are the professors of theology in our two faculties of theology, those responsible for the information service, youth work or the fostering of biblical awareness in local congregations, etc. There is no limit to the list of these different ministries.

Whether collegial or personal, each ministry is inaugurated by a service of recognition, with laying on of hands and *epiclesis*. I should return to this later on. First, let me outline its significance.

Ministry is not ministry because it is said to be so by the Church but because individuals or groups are called by the Spirit and enabled to carry out the designated service of Christ and humankind. That is why it is essential that the spiritual nature of ministry be expressed in an appropriate manner. Our National Synod has approved an order of service for the Recognition of Ministries which contains these elements: an undertaking by ministers to be faithful servants of the Lord in the exercise of their charge, followed by the laying on of hands, and a prayer that the Spirit will enable them to accomplish their tasks. The set words for the commitment and *epiclesis* vary according to the ministry into which the person concerned is entering.

At the time of the Reformation, the ceremony was called 'the laying on of hands'. In the nineteenth and for most of the twentieth centuries, the usual term was 'consecration'. The word 'ordination' was unpopular, because to French Protestant ears it had priestly overtones; it seemed to imply a Roman Catholic understanding of the rite, whereby a person was empowered to perform the transubstantiation of bread and wine at the Mass. Then again, partly through our dialogue with Lutherans, some have advocated the use of the term 'ordination', claiming that the word 'consecration' is better suited to the celebration of baptism than the setting apart of a minister. This argument, though, does not suffice to counter the feeling that 'ordination' has specifically Roman Catholic overtones. So, rather than prolong such linguistic arguments, the Synod decided that for the moment we would talk of 'recognition of ministries'. But it should be understood, and we firmly insist on this, that our service of recognition is exactly the same, and is to be understood in precisely the same way, as the service which all the other churches of the Reformation designate by the term ordination. When I was President of the National Council, I wrote a letter to this effect to the President of the Leuenberg Church Fellowship, who had written to us to ask what the meaning of the decisions of our Synod was.

Ministers are only recognized once. When they change situations, their service of induction, or welcome as we prefer to call it, recalls the service of recognition but does not repeat it. A retired minister remains a minister and therefore is subject to our *Discipline*. But we no longer require of ordained ministers that they remain in active service for life. What is essential for us is that they remain faithful to the service of the Lord. Now ministers do not have the monopoly of this, so we make it possible for those who give up their ministry to take another job. It can sometimes happen that the church terminates the ministry of a person who is obviously not suitable for it.

We consider that it is also very important that the ministry of councils be recognized. They are entitled to assume responsibility in the government of the church not because they are elected by a church meeting or a synod, but because of the prayer of the church that the Spirit guide them in the exercise of their responsibilities. I shall explain in my paper on *episcope* in the Reformed Church of France what responsibilities devolve to the Regional Council and its president, and how they have in fact, even if the word itself is not mentioned, a real ministry of *episcope*, amongst their other duties.

A lay person can be called to preside over Sunday services, if need be including the Lord's Supper, a baptism or funeral. This happens each Sunday in the Reformed Church of France. Following unification in 1938, it was decided to adopt the Methodist practice of lay preachers. We have therefore made it possible for our regional councils to license such people. They receive training at local or regional level. They are not ministers of the Reformed Church of France.

Ministry in the French Lutheran Churches

André Birmelé

The two French Lutheran churches, the ECAAL (the Church of the Augsburg Confession of Alsace and Lorraine) and the EELF (the Evangelical–Lutheran Church of France), have the same understanding of ministry as the majority of Lutheran churches worldwide.

The Church and the Ministry of Word and Sacrament

The Church is the assembly of all believers, to whom the gospel is faithfully preached and the holy sacraments administered according to the gospel (Augsburg Confession, 7). Through word and sacraments, God gives his grace to human beings, justifies them and makes them members of the community of believers. For this gospel to become earthed, God has given his Church 'a ministry whose task it is to teach the gospel and make the sacraments available' (Augsburg Confession, 5). The ministry of public proclamation of the gospel and the administration of the sacraments is fundamental and essential for the Church.

On the basis of this theological conviction, the French Lutheran churches understand ministry not as a simple structural given, of the type that is indispensable to every human organization, but as an integral part of the word that constitutes the Church. They emphasize nonetheless that it is the ministry of proclamation of the gospel through word and sacraments that is constitutive of the Church and not a particular form of this ministry that has developed in the Church over the years.

Universal Priesthood and Ordained Ministry

The ministry of the Church is primarily entrusted to the whole community. Each member is called by baptism to witness to Jesus Christ.

Specific members, however, are called, trained and ordained, to ensure that the gospel is publicly proclaimed, to celebrate the sacraments, to ensure that there is teaching, and to have pastoral charge of a local community.

The EELF and the ECAAL both consider it important that this particular service should always be seen in the context of the universal priesthood of the community and that it should always continue to serve the community. The ministry which is entrusted to a person at ordination, however, should not be confused with universal priesthood. Ministers share with the parish Presbyteral Council in the leadership of the local community; and in this respect they participate in the universal priesthood of the whole local community, which they also represent to the wider Church. But these same ministers are also the ambassadors of the universal Church to a local situation. They not only represent the local to the wider Church, but also the wider to the local. To indicate the necessary tension between the local community and the universal Church, no parish may elect a minister without the agreement of the church at regional level. And conversely, no minister may be allocated to a situation without the agreement of the local community. This two-way movement expresses the catholicity of the Church.

The French Lutheran churches insist that every minister who is publicly charged with the ministry of word and sacraments must be ordained. Every one of their pastors who exercises such a ministry is ordained. Every person on pastoral placement is ordained at the very latest on the day that they take charge of a local community.

Ordination to this particular ministry is based on a particular mission entrusted by Christ who calls men and women to be set apart to the service of the gospel and the faith. This ordination is not the locus of any divine grace other than that which is conferred by the word, baptism and eucharist. Ordination does not confer on ministers any capacity other than that which is enjoyed by every person who has been baptized. Their functions in the Church, however, are quite different. Ordination is their public recognition by the Church, which confers on them a threefold mission: preaching the gospel, celebrating the sacraments, and having pastoral responsibility in the name of the universal Church, which institutes them as ministers of the Church. Ordination is always presided over by the Ecclesiastical Inspector (see below) and invokes the gift of the Holy Spirit through the laying on of hands and the promises of the Church and the candidate. It is not linked to a specific geographical location. The responsibility of a particular community, with mutual undertakings by the pastor and the local community, dates from the induction. Induction, unlike ordination, is linked to a specific time and place, and is repeated when there is a change of post. The EELF and the ECAAL insist on the distinction between ordination and induction.

The Threefold Ministry

The EELF and the ECAAL have always been familiar with the threefold form of ministry as it developed during the history of the Church. They see it as an important structural means of expressing particular ministries. An enriching gift from God, this expression is nonetheless relative. It is the fruit of historical evolution, and thereby one possible translation of the ministry of the Church. There could be other ways of understanding and organizing ministry. The fact remains, however, that the threefold form: ministry of oversight (*episcope*), pastor and deacon is still the norm today in the French Lutheran churches.

There is a current difficulty in defining diaconal ministry, which assumes very different forms in practice. For many years, it was taken for granted that diaconal ministry was concerned with social responsibility (cf., for example, the deaconesses) or with pastoral and liturgical matters. In this latter respect, deacons were often seen as pastoral auxiliaries, with the responsibility of helping ministers in the exercise of their functions. Such a ministry was often devalued and unrecognized. Nowadays efforts are being made to define more satisfactorily this essential form of ministry. Training courses are being offered for Sunday School teachers, readers, deacons, etc. In many instances the assumption of such ministry leads to ordination. While this should not be confused with the ordination of a minister, this ordination is the recognition by the regional church of a particular vocation, an undertaking, a laying on of hands, and a sending out in mission. It is indicated for those who have a diaconal ministry and whom the Church entrusts with the preaching of the gospel, even the administration of the sacraments, but who do not have pastoral charge of a community (preachers, parish visitors).

The Ministry of Oversight (*Episcope*)

The mission of leadership of the community is part of the ministry of the Church. This mission does not fall to the ordained minister alone; it is incumbent on the whole community. Provision is made for the leadership of the parish and the church at regional level without relying solely on the ministry of the ordained.

The French Lutheran churches have an episcopal-synodical form of government. At all levels of leadership there is a certain tension between synodical government and ordained ministers. This is the case in the local community (encounters between pastor and presbyteral council) and at regional level, where decisions arise out of discussions in the Directorate (in the case of the ECAAL) or the Executive Council (in the case of the EELF), between the elected representatives of the Synod and the Ecclesiastical Inspectors (*episcope*). At this level of church government, in each of the two churches, there is a lay president.

The episcopal function is served by the Ecclesiastical Inspectors (two in the EELF and seven in the ECAAL). Each has specific responsibility for a particular region. They exercise this particular ministry together and in a manner that is personal, collegial and communal. They have regular meetings at a regional level in the case both of the EELF and the ECAAL, and at national level.

The Ecclesiastical Inspector is the *pastor pastorum* for a region. He alone may ordain to the pastoral ministry. His is a ministry of unity, of advice and of visitation, a ministry of oversight and of pastoral responsibility within an Inspection. (In the ECAAL, that means 35 local parishes; the EELF distinguishes between the Inspections of Paris and Montbéliard.) The Ecclesiastical Inspector is elected for five or seven years by the Assembly of the Inspection, which consists of the lay representatives and ministers of the local communities in the Inspection. He is officially inducted into his functions by the other Ecclesiastical Inspectors. This episcopal ministry is entrusted to him for a certain time; it is a particular form of the ordained ministry of word and sacraments.

Both the EELF and the ECAAL attach great importance to the way in which the ministry of the whole Church is exercised among them. They experience the richness of their episcopal-synodical structures, while being quite aware that their particular form of government is historically relative and therefore secondary to the unique charge of mission and ministry which God has entrusted to his Church in this world.

Episcope in the Reformed Church of France

Jean-Pierre Monsarrat

The ecclesiastical documents that are authoritative for the Reformed Church of France are the following:

> *Les statuts de l'Union Nationale*: Under French law, any body (society, charity, church, etc. . . .) which wants to be a legal entity must define its purpose and organization in statutes that are registered by the State. The *Église Réformée de France* defines itself in its statutes as a church whose faith is set forth in

> *La Declaration de Foi*: The word 'declaration' is used instead of 'confession' because when it was drawn up and passed by the National Synod in 1938 it was not understood as replacing the *Confessio Gallicana* of 1559.

> *La Discipline de l'Église Réformée*, the body of rules that define the workings of the Reformed Church of France. When the National Synod introduces a new arrangement for the life of the church or the work of its ministers, it is included in the *Discipline* so that it can be enforced. In a way the *Discipline* is the body of canons of the *Église Réformée*.

> *La Liturgie de l'Église Réformée*, for the worship of the church, and *La Liturgie de Reconnaissance des Ministères et des Ministres*, our Ordinal.

To define what is the *episcope* in the *Église Réformée de France*, one has to refer to what is said about oversight in the above documents.

Two Remarks on the Polity of the *Église Réformée*

● The Continental churches know nothing of the Westminster Assembly. The French Reformed system of church government has its origins in the sixteenth-century *Discipline*, with very important contributions from the nineteenth and twentieth centuries.

- The preamble to the *Discipline* asserts that the reality of the Church is in the local congregations of the faithful and *also*, and it could be added *equally*, 'in the assemblies of those churches' on a national (or regional or international) level. Therefore one should not be surprised to find the word 'church' in the singular used to cover a small congregation, in the same way Paul wrote to the church in Corinth or in Rome, as well as the Reformed Church as a whole.

An Outline of How the Ministry of Oversight is Exercised in the *Église Réformée*

One must start with the Église locale, the local church (which is what the *Discipline*, in accordance with its preamble, calls what is generally termed the congregation or parish). Each local church is under the direct rule of the *Conseil presbytéral*, elected by the General Assembly. The members of the Presbyteral Council are elected for a six-year term and half of them come to the end of their term every three years. The Council, and not the Assembly, leads the life of the congregation. Its ministry is 'recognized' or acknowledged in a service which includes a commitment and the laying on of hands with a prayer invoking the Holy Spirit. The minister(s) is (are) *ex officio* member(s) of the Council, and take(s) part in its work as partner(s) of those that are elected by the local church. The minister(s), as 'pastor(s) of the Reformed Church of France' is (are) called to 'gather the Christian community around the Word of God and in the celebration of Baptism and the Lord's Supper, . . . with the Presbyteral Council, to serve the unity of the Body of Christ and its mission . . .'

A local church can be a diocese in itself due to the way its membership is scattered in *ecclesiolae* far apart. The ministries of Council and pastor have, then, an important overtone of *episcope*. The pastoral ministry has often been considered by Reformed theologians as that of a bishop, because of his responsibility in the oversight of the life of the church and the *ecclesiolae*, with the various ministries active throughout, entrusted to him.

All the Local Churches Are Part of One of the Eight Regions that Make Up the *Église Réformée*

Each region is governed by a Synod (at least half its membership lay persons) that meets once (a long weekend) or twice (a weekend and an additional day) a year and appoints, for a three-year term, a Regional Council. The Moderator of the Synod plays his or her part only during the Synod meetings. The Council elects its officers and among them the President.

The ministry of oversight is the responsibility of the Regional Council as such. Its ministry is acknowledged in a service which includes a commitment, and a prayer invoking the Holy Spirit with laying on of hands. The corporate ministry of the Council is described as taking care of the churches of the region, visiting and encouraging them, helping the weak and those that are in difficulty, and tightening the bonds that unite them all.

Oversight is also the particular 'office and responsibility' of the Regional President. The presidency is a full-time ministry entrusted to a pastor. Most presidents serve for an average of three, sometimes four, terms. The President 'is to show in a personal ministry the pastoral character of the authority in his region. He leads the work of the Council. He can at all times visit a church, meet a minister or summon him'. He can take part in any meeting of a presbyteral council. The eight presidents are all members *ex officio* of the National Synod. They meet five or six times a year, their main concern being then to establish which churches are in need of finding a minister, which ministers ought to be called to a new incumbency and which are seeking one, and to advise the presbyteral councils and the ministers in their choice. No minister can be appointed without their taking part in the process of decision. The Regional Council must give its approval to an appointment.

The Eight Regional Synods Elect Some of their Members (Half Lay) to Make Up the National Synod

The National Synod meets once a year in a three-day session. It is *the* governing body of the church. Every three years it elects a National Council which, in turn, elects its officers and among them a full-time president.

The ministry of the National Council is also acknowledged during a service in which there is a commitment and laying on of hands with a prayer for the Spirit. The Council is said to be in the service of the unity of the church and of its mission, of its faithfulness to the Lord, of its openness to all. It is in charge of leading the church as a whole and exercising a general oversight.

The full-time president of the National Council, who is also a pastor, has an important part in the carrying out of that ministry, but the personal character of his office is not as well defined and stressed in the 'canons' of the church as that of the President of the Regional Council.

The Work and Pronouncements of the National Synod on the Matter of *Episcope*

In 1964 the National Synod took an important decision on the 'devolution of authority and authority at the regional level'. The synod stated that the 'authority of the pastoral ministry belongs in matters pertaining to teaching to the synod which is enabled to say what is the faith and the discipline of the church, in its episcopal aspect to the Regional Council which is called to be the effective leader of the church, and in its pastoral dimension to the President of the Regional Council when he practises the *paraclesis* (exhortation, consolation) of the church'.

Since then the Synods have devoted a lot of time to the matter of ministry but have not changed what was decided in 1964 relating to the exercise of authority.

When discussing the *BEM* document in 1985 the National Synod made no remarks (which does not mean it gave its approval!) on the particular topic of oversight.

Concerning the Threefold Ministry

The *Église Réformée* has often stressed, since the end of the 1940s, the diversity of ministries. The idea was to change the way in which the pastors monopolized all the responsibilities and activities in the church, denying in practice the priesthood of all believers which they were teaching.

The diversity of ministries has been understood in different ways. At first (during the 1950s) there was an attempt to create something like an order of deacons. But it soon became apparent that a subordinate ministry was so contrary to the traditional idea in the Reformed Church that all ministers are equal, that the attempt had to be given up.

The Synod, at the beginning of the eighties, chose another way of promoting the diversity of ministries. It is now understood as meaning different sorts of activities in the service of the gospel according to the different gifts of each one and the different needs of the mission and *diakonia* of the Church. The primary importance of the ministry of word and sacrament is maintained.

Diversity is also understood as meaning personal ministries on the one hand, corporate or collegial ministries on the other. A member of a local or a regional council is not a minister; he only takes part in the corporate ministry of the council of which he is a member. All personal and corporate ministries are 'recognized' or acknowledged in a service which includes an appropriate commitment, laying on of hands and invocation of the Holy Spirit for the particular gifts requested for each specific ministry.

Theses on Ordination

The question of ministries and ordination has often been a source of internal and bilateral conflict in our French Reformed and Lutheran churches. In the name of these churches, Jean Bosc and Albert Greiner drew up the following Theses in 1961. They have been submitted to the respective synods for approval.

A preliminary remark:

The term traditionally used in the Reformed churches of France is 'consecration'. The Lutheran churches speak of 'ordination'. The latter term is preferred here because it seemed more comprehensive. 'Consecration', in fact, seems to imply 'sacralization'. 'Ordination', on the other hand, indicates a precise place and a determined function in the Order of the Church, that is to say, in the diversity and articulation of its unity. In addition, the word 'ordination' is the more universally employed in the ecumenical world.

1. The Lord Jesus Christ, living in and for his body which is the Church, gives it diverse ministries so that it may be built up in him and accomplish in the world the mission for which he has destined it. So it is he who calls, by the action of the Holy Spirit, to any particular ministry of the Church. The origin of this vocation is hidden. Those who receive it respond in faith and declare that they are ready to assume responsibility for the ministry to which the Lord is calling them.

    That does not prevent the Church, rightly preoccupied with carrying out its mission, from discerning the gifts that have been given and externalizing that inner vocation.

2. At all events, it is for the Church, in obedience to its Lord and drawing on the wisdom it has been given, to recognize the vocation in its midst. Without claiming to be the final arbiter of the authenticity of such vocations, it tries to discern the signs. It is also incumbent on the Church to give the ministers it has been granted appropriate training; and this training will also test their vocation. Last of all, it is the Church that ordains them to ministry, that is,

introduces each to a designated function. And this is done according to the prescriptions of the Book of Order (*Discipline*).

3. The ceremony of ordination is the public liturgical act during which
    the Christian community recognizes ministers, institutes them in
    their charge, and with laying on of hands invokes the enabling
    power of the Holy Spirit upon them. As they do this, ministers
    already in pastoral charge receive the newly ordained into their
    ministry with the approbation of all the people in the Church. And
    the people recognize in them the responsibilities and authority
    linked with this charge.

4. Solemn ordination does not constitute an action by which power is
    transmitted by ministers in pastoral charge to the newly ordained
    through a material succession. Nor does the act of ordination intro-
    duce the persons who are its object to a clerical state that would
    distinguish them from the people in the Church; it does not confer
    a particular character. The Lord Jesus Christ is the sole source of
    ministerial authority, and that, whatever it is, is a function of the
    whole Church, entrusted in a particular manner to one member of
    the community.

    New ministers are welcomed in obedience to the Lord Jesus Christ,
    and in the expectation that his gifts will be conferred. It is true to
    say that those who receive the ministers into their order recognize
    that these have joined the succession of ministers of the Church
    guaranteed by the faithfulness of Jesus Christ.

    As the Church, with laying on of hands, invokes the assistance of
    the Holy Spirit for new ministers, it believes and affirms by virtue
    of the promise it has received, that the Lord grants and will grant
    this assistance.

5. This ordination and its liturgical manifestation are the norm for every
    recognized ministry of the Church. By ministry, we must not under-
    stand any gift or any activity that may take place in the Christian
    community. The term is precise; it refers to the different services that
    rely on the gifts of the Lord and which give rise to those permanent
    functions that are necessary for the life and mission of the Church. It
    is for the Church to recognize and define such ministries.

6.   Public ordination is celebrated by a minister who is authorized in accordance with the Order of the Church, in the presence of and in communion with representatives of all the ministries of the Church and the whole people of God.

Decisions of the Church

The National Synod of the Reformed Church of France – Valence, 1961 (decisions XIII and XIV)

The National Synod is delighted that a common study has been undertaken by representatives of ECAAL, EELF, ERAL and ERF, with the intention of drawing up a liturgical text for consecration and ordination. It sees that as a sign which commits it to pursuing with greater fervour the unity of the Protestant churches in France. It requests the National Council to do all that is in its power to encourage collaboration with the representatives of these churches in the pursuit of studies on matters of ministry.

It receives with gratitude the 'Theses on Ordination' by Bosc and Greiner. Without going into detailed discussion, it states that these are in fundamental agreement with the faith and order texts that are authoritative for the Reformed Church of France.

It wishes this document to be used in the conversations with the Lutheran churches on ordination.

It recommends it to the commissions of the Reformed Church of France which are preparing studies on ministry and ministries.

ECAAL, EELF and ERAL

The three churches do not seem to have made a formal response to the Bosc–Greiner text. But these Theses on Ordination have been used as a basic text in the study, adoption and practice of the 'Liturgy of welcome for ministers of the Church' (in particular for the Reformed Church of Alsace and Lorraine, Synod of Hagondange, 1975 (decision 18)).

[Extract from: *Accords et Dialogues Oecumeniques*, by A. Birmelé and J. Terme (Les Bergers et les Mages, 1995)]

Index